T0345306

Terence O'Neill

HISTORICAL ASSOCIATION OF IRELAND

LIFE AND TIMES

NEW SERIES

General Editor: Ciaran Brady

Now available
Michael Davitt by Carla King
Thomas Kettle by Senia Pašeta
John Mitchel by James Quinn
Denis Guiney by Peter Costello
Frank Ryan by Fearghal McGarry
William Martin Murphy by Thomas J. Morrissey, SJ
Justin McCarthy by Eugene J. Doyle
Charles Stewart Parnell by Alan O'Day
Terence O'Neill by Marc Mulholland

Titles are in preparation on Isaac Butt, Desmond Fitzgerald
and Maria Edgeworth.

Terence O'Neill

MARC MULHOLLAND

✦

Published on behalf of
the Historical Association of Ireland
by

UNIVERSITY COLLEGE DUBLIN PRESS
Preas Choláiste Ollscoile Bhaile Átha Cliath
2013

First published 2013 on behalf of the
Historical Association of Ireland by
University College Dublin Press

© Marc Mulholland, 2013

ISBN 978-1-906359-75-1
ISSN 2009-1397

University College Dublin Press
Newman House, 86 St Stephen's Green
Dublin 2, Ireland
www.ucdpress.ie

All rights reserved. No part of this publication
may be reproduced, stored in a retrieval system,
or transmitted in any form or by any means, electronic,
photocopying, recording or otherwise without
the prior permission of the publisher.

*The right of Marc Mulholland to be identified as
the author of this work has been asserted by him*

Cataloguing in Publication data available from the British Library

Typeset in Scotland in Ehrhardt by Ryan Shiels
Text design by Lyn Davies
Printed in England on acid-free paper by
Antony Rowe, Chippenham, Wilts.

CONTENTS

Foreword   *vii*
Preface   *viii*
Chronology of O'Neill's Life and Times   *x*

1   The Making of the Politician   *1*

2   Into the Premiership   *21*

3   O'Neillism and Paisleyism   *37*

4   O'Neill's PEP Pill   *51*

5   The North Explodes   *58*

6   Legacy   *86*

Notes   *98*
Select Bibliography   *112*
Index   *115*

Dedicated to my Parents, Dominic and Ita

*

FOREWORD

Originally conceived over a decade ago to place the lives of leading figures in Irish history against the background of new research on the problems and conditions of their times and modern assessments of their historical significance, the Historical Association of Ireland Life and Times series enjoyed remarkable popularity and success. A second series has now been planned in association with UCD Press in a new format and with fuller scholarly apparatus. Encouraged by the reception given to the earlier series, the volumes in the new series will be expressly designed to be of particular help to students preparing for the Leaving Certificate, for GCE Advanced Level and for undergraduate history courses as well as appealing to the happily insatiable appetite for new views of Irish history among the general public.

CIARAN BRADY
Historical Association of Ireland

PREFACE

Terence O'Neill was Prime Minister at Stormont when Northern Ireland entered the thirty-year crisis known as the Troubles. He is remembered as a well-meaning if rather timid and ineffectual liberal who blundered into disaster. There was more to him than that, however. O'Neill's thinking could be extraordinarily ambitious. This was a man who proposed draining Lough Neagh to create a seventh Northern Ireland county, recommended his 'Programme to Enlist the People' as an international solution to the youth rebellion of 1968, and considered standing for the post of President of the Irish Republic. O'Neill was not just another of the crusty 'fur coat brigade' who had for years dominated Ulster. From a long line of protestant defenders of the Irish link to Britain, he was nonetheless intensely proud of his descent from the ancient Gaelic clan of O Neill. He fought bravely for crown and country in wartime, and led the Ulster Unionist Party in peacetime, but ultimately believed that a united self-governing Ireland was one day inevitable.

In this short book I argue that O'Neill was much more audacious than has generally been depicted. He developed a sophisticated analysis of division within Northern Ireland and set in train ambitious schemes – Civic weeks and PEP – to moderate them. A true believer in greater fairness, O'Neill defied extraordinary pressure from Paisleyites and much of his own party to introduce real if limited reform even before the civil rights movement erupted in 1968. In the last months of his premiership, with extraordinary boldness, he attempted to break the mould of protestant versus catholic politics in Northern Ireland, even at the price of splitting his own party. O'Neill's ambitions, and their failure, deserve serious re-consideration.

This book, of course, concentrates on O'Neill. But it also takes into account three other men committed, each in their own way, to defending the honourable estate of the British in Ulster: Brian Faulkner, William Craig and Ian Paisley. All four were born within twelve years of each other. The landmark decade of the 1960s made them, and they did much to make modern Northern Ireland. Their careers were intertwined in life, and they do so here.

I should like to thank all at UCD Press for taking this project on, particularly Noelle Moran and Ciaran Brady. I have discussed its contents with the 150 or so students who have taken the Northern Ireland Special Subject at the University of Oxford over these past dozen years. I am grateful to them all.

A note on terminology: I use 'Unionist' when referring to the Ulster Unionist Party or its members, 'unionist' when referring to the wider British protestant community in Northern Ireland. 'Derry' and 'Londonderry' are used interchangeably for the same city.

MARC MULHOLLAND
August 2013

CHRONOLOGY OF O'NEILL'S LIFE
AND TIMES

1914
10 September Terence O'Neill born.
6 November Capt. Hon. Arthur O'Neill, Terence's father, first MP to be killed in the War.

1921
June Northern Ireland comes into existence; Ireland partitioned.

1922
9 February Terence's mother remarries.
20 May Shane's Castle, O'Neill family 'Big House', burnt by IRA.

1936
O'Neill spends a year in France and Austria.

1939
Second World War breaks out. O'Neill joins the Irish Guards.

1940
14 May Capt. Hon. Brian O'Neill killed in action.

1944
4 February Terence marries Jean Whitaker.
September Terence injured near Nijmegan in Holland.
24 October Lt. Col. Shane O'Neill killed in action.

1945

8 May German surrender.

Terence O'Neill and family move to Ahoghill, Co. Antrim, Northern Ireland.

1946

7 November O'Neill elected unopposed as Ulster Unionist Party MP for Bannside, Co. Antrim.

1947

O'Neill makes maiden speech in Stormont on the Education Act.

1948–53

O'Neill Parliamentary Secretary to the Ministry of Health.

1949

19 February 'Chapel Gate Election' in Northern Ireland. Brian Faulkner elected for East Down.

18 April Southern Ireland becomes a republic.

2 June Ireland Act receives Royal Assent. Stipulates no unification of Ireland without the consent of the Parliament of Northern Ireland.

1953–56

O'Neill Deputy Speaker at Stormont.

1956

O'Neill joins cabinet as Minister of Home Affairs.

12 December IRA launches 'Operation Harvest', better known as the 'Border Campaign'.

1956–63

O'Neill Minister of Finance.

1962

26 February IRA calls off 'Operation Harvest' for lack of support.

23 October Publication of 'Hall Report' marks bankruptcy of Unionist economic strategy.

29 November O'Neill delivers 'Pottinger Speech'.

1963

26 February 'Matthew report' proposes modernisation of Northern Ireland's infrastructure.

23 March O'Neill invited to replace Lord Brookeborough as Prime Minister.

25 March William Craig, Chief Whip, organises poll of Unionist MPs approving O'Neill as leader.

5 April O'Neill announces intention to literally 'transform the face of Ulster'.

23 October O'Neill presents 'Wilson Plan' on Economic Development.

1964

24 April O'Neill visits a Roman Catholic school; first Unionist leader to do so.

13 May O'Neill secretly briefs Unionist MPs on plans to make County Armagh 'New City' securely protestant and Unionist.

30 June Government recognises Northern Ireland Committee of Irish Congress of Trade Unions.

28 September 'Divis street riots' over flying of Irish tri-colour flag in west Belfast.

1 October O'Neill announces that he is in favour of 'bridge-building' between the two communities.

1965

1 January New Ministry of Development and Ministry of Health and Social Services come into effect.

14 January O'Neill meets Sean Lemass, Taoiseach of Ireland, at Stormont.

15 January Paisley launches 'O'Neill Must Go' campaign.

8 May Unionist 'faceless men' exposed as lobbying against investment in majority-catholic Londonderry.

6 July Controversial name of 'Craigavon' chosen for New City.

25 November General election a major defeat for the Northern Ireland Labour Party and increases Unionist majority by four.

1966

April Illegal nationalist commemorations of Easter 1916 Rising pass off peacefully.

9 April O'Neill addresses Corrymeela Conference on 'The Ulster Community'.

6 June Paisleyites picket Presbyterian General Assembly in Belfast.

28 June Following murders, O'Neill bans loyalist Ulster Volunteer Force under the Special Powers Act.

4 July Queen Elizabeth II visits Belfast, fails to support O'Neill's 'bridge-building'.

18 July Paisley imprisoned. Riots follow.

3 August At a 10 Downing Street summit, Labour Prime Minister Harold Wilson puts pressure on O'Neill to speed up reform.

23 September Rumours emerge of Unionist petition, signed by at least 12 of 36 MPs, in favour of O'Neill stepping down.

27 September O'Neill wins vote of confidence from the Parliamentary Unionist party.

8 October In cabinet reshuffle, William Craig demoted to Minister of Home Affairs.

13 December O'Neill announces reform to increase funding for Roman Catholic Mater Hospital.

16 December Westminster constituency boundaries for Belfast re-drawn, with no pro-Unionist gerrymander.

1967

23 January O'Neill announces cross-community 'Civic weeks' and 'Programme to Enlist the People' (PEP).

29 January Northern Ireland Civil Rights Association (NICRA) established.

26 April Harry West dismissed from the cabinet over the St. Angelo affair.

1968

20 February O'Neill defends strategy of 'action in words'.

23 May State funding increased for Voluntary (Roman Catholic) Schools.

5 October Civil Rights demonstration attacked by RUC police in Derry.

9 October 2000 students march from University to City Hall. Sit-down protest as Paisleyites block route.

16 October Sit-down demonstration in Derry for civil rights.

16 November 15,000 march for civil rights in Derry.

22 November Government announces Five Point Reform Programme.

30 November Paisleyites occupy cathedral city of Armagh.

9 December O'Neill broadcasts to the province – 'Ulster is at a Crossroads'.

11 December O'Neill sacks William Craig, Minister of Home affairs. Receives vote of confidence from Ulster Unionist MPs.

1969

4 January People's Democracy march attacked by loyalists at Burntollet Bridge. Rioting in Derry.

13 January Civil rights marchers turn violent in Newry.

15 January Government announces a Commission of Inquiry, to be headed up by Lord Cameron.

24 January Brian Faulkner resigns from cabinet.

3 February 'Portadown Parliament' of dissident Unionist MPs call for O'Neill's resignation.

4 February O'Neill calls a General election.

24 February General Election fails to bolster O'Neill's position.

18 April People's Democracy candidate Bernadette Devlin wins Mid-Ulster seat with nationalist and republican support.

21 April Loyalists bomb Belfast water supplies.

23 April Unionist MPs accept 'one man one vote' in local government elections. James Chichester-Clarke resigns from cabinet.

28 April O'Neill announces resignation as leader of Ulster Unionist Party and Prime Minister.

1 May James Chichester-Clarke succeeds O'Neill, defeating Brian Faulkner.

14 August Following serious rioting in Derry and Belfast, British army deploys to streets of Northern Ireland.

October Ulster at the Crossroads, a collection of O'Neill's speeches, published.

1970

1 January O'Neill made life peer. Ultimately takes title, Lord O'Neill of the Maine.

16 April Paisley wins Bannside seat vacated by O'Neill.

1971–2

O'Neill advertises willingness to stand for presidency of the Irish republic.

1972

23 April O'Neill appointed to the Board of Guardians of the National Gallery of Ireland.

7 November O'Neill's autobiography published.

22 November O'Neill leaves the Orange order.

1973–4

Sunningdale Agreement on power-sharing and 'Irish dimension' negotiated and collapses. O'Neill concludes that middle-class leadership has failed.

1990

13 June O'Neill dies.

CHAPTER I

The Making of the Politician

O'Neill's lineage can be reliably traced back to a Gaelic Prince killed in battle in 1283, and Dod's peerage whimsically went further back to Niall of the Nine Hostages, High King of Ireland from c. 379 to c. 409 AD, and far beyond. O'Neill was not a direct descendant of these Ulster kings, however. His family indirectly descended from the O'Neills of Clanaboy, a branch founded by a nominee of the English after the 'Flight of the Earls' (1607), when 'Red' Hugh Ó Néill fled to the continent with his compatriots following a failed rebellion against the Crown. Terence was actually descended from Edward Chichester, an immigrant to Ulster from Devonshire in England, whose brother, Sir Arthur Chichester, had been Lord Deputy since 1604 and as such Red Hugh's chief opponent.

From his residence in Carrickfergus, Sir Arthur Chichester oversaw the Planation of Ulster scheme, which founded the protestant bulwark in Ulster on immigrants from Scotland and England. His niece, Mary, married Sir Henry O'Neill at Randalstown, and they had a daughter, Rose. Father and daughter spent much of their years at Whitehall in London and there they struck up friendships with the Royal Family. The O'Neills of Clanaboy were granted a Baronetcy by Charles I for gallantry at Edgehill in 1642, the first pitched battle of the Civil War between crown and parliament. When Princess Mary of England married the prince of

Orange in 1641, Rose O'Neill went to the Dutch Republic as companion and lady-in-waiting. She helped to raise the man attributed with securing the protestant succession in Britain and Ireland when he seized the British throne in the Glorious Revolution of 1688: William III.

The eighteenth-century O'Neills were amongst the wealthiest landed families in County Antrim. In 1761, John O'Neill was returned to the Irish Parliament for the family seat of Randalstown. He was a 'patriot', an opponent of the anti-catholic Penal Laws, and a prominent member of the paramilitary Irish Volunteers. Though associated with separatist United Irishmen through the Whig Club, he was loyal to the Crown and in 1793 was raised to the peerage. Upon hearing of the United Irishmen rising in the north in June 1798, he raised troops and rushed to Antrim town, where he fell before rebel pikes. Though lifted bodily with his horse into Antrim Castle, he died of his wounds eleven days later. John's heir, Charles, refused ever after to set foot in Antrim town. Unlike his father, Charles was a strong supporter of the parliamentary Union between Great Britain and Ireland, and was one of the first peers to sit in the United Kingdom House of Lords formed in 1801. An enthusiastic Orangeman, he rose to become Grand Master of this protestant Order. His son in turn, Charles Henry, as an MP opposed both Catholic Emancipation and Repeal of the Union. Charles Henry never married and so he willed his estates to William Chichester, his second cousin twice removed and a fifth-generation Church of Ireland clergyman, who in 1855 by royal licence took the name O'Neill. William was married into the Torrens family, whose luminaries included an Anglican Archdeacon of Dublin and Sir Henry Torrens, Adjutant General to Forces, a veteran of the Battle of Waterloo, and military secretary to King William IV. William was raised to the peerage as Baron O'Neill in 1868.

William's son, Robert Torrens O'Neill, sat as a Conservative MP for Mid-Antrim from 1885 to 1910. His nephew, Arthur O'Neill, succeeded to the seat in 1910, now effectively as an Ulster Unionist MP vehemently opposed to the nationalist campaign for a devolved Home Rule parliament in Ireland. He was unusual in having married across the wide divide that had opened up between Unionists and nationalist Home Rulers. In 1902, Robert married Lady Annabel, daughter of the 1st Marquess of Crewe. Crewe had been appointed Lord Lieutenant of Ireland when the Liberal administration of 1892 to 1895 had tried to put Home Rule on the statue book. Arthur participated in the Ulster Unionist campaign against the Third Home Rule Bill of 1912, which promised an all-Ireland devolution parliament, and (as a military veteran of the Boer War) he helped organise the anti-nationalist Ulster Volunteer Force in the Ballymena area. Still, he was a rather unwilling politician, and when the First World War broke out was quick to join his 2nd Life Guards regiment.

In 1966, when restive Unionist MPs were challenging Terence O'Neill's right to lead as Prime Minister, the conservative *Unionist* newspaper ran an article on 'The O'Neill's of Antrim' to assert his loyalist bona fides:

On both sides of his family the Prime Minister can prove an unbroken protestant descent for 360 years. The O'Neills resisted the 1798 rebellion, voted for the Act of Union, and were leaders of the Orange Order. The Chichesters came over from England and served both Queen Elizabeth and King James I – the man who planted Ulster with protestants, while in later generations they provided an almost unparalleled line of protestant clergymen. The Prime Minister's father drilled the Ulster Volunteers in 1912 and was the first Member of Parliament to be killed in the service of his county in 1914. Both the Prime Minister's brothers were killed in the last war and he himself was wounded in Holland. It would be hard to prove a greater loyalty for a greater length of time in many other families.[1]

Terence O'Neill certainly took pride in his protestant genealogy, but he also made much of his 'Gaelic' inheritance to indicate his acceptability to catholics. The most exaggerated claim features on the dust-cover of his autobiography: 'O'Neill bore an Irish name, not one of English or Scottish inheritance, and could claim direct descent from the kings of Ireland. Thus to catholics, he was more than just a Prime Minister.' But really, his loyalty was to a tradition close to its last legs in Ireland even as his life began. It was no doubt with a mischievous smile when, in 1972, he identified himself with two radical-left pro-Irish nationalist ornaments of the aristocracy: '[T]he rebel Countess, Countess Markievicz, was, like the noble Earl, Lord Longford, and myself, of impeccable Anglo–Irish descent.'[2] O'Neill was intensely proud of the 'Red Hand of Ulster', a symbol found on Northern Ireland's provincial flag, but was always quick to remind listeners that it was a symbol of the O'Neill clan, Europe's oldest traceable aristocratic family. When in 1982, Jorge O'Neill, a Portuguese noble and distant scion of the Gaelic earls, was inaugurated chieftain of all the O'Neills, Terence was in proud attendance.

YOUTH

Terence was born on 10 September 1914. The youngest of five children, he was given the second name 'Marne' to commemorate the contemporary World War One battle. He was only three months old when his father became the first MP of the Great War to be killed in action, aged 38.[3] Terence's uncle, later Lord Rathcavan, took his father's place at Westminster and sat as an MP for a record 35 years continuous service, becoming Father of the House in

1951. From 1921 Rathcavan served simultaneously in the Northern Ireland House of Commons, set up to administer the internal affairs of the six United Kingdom counties of Northern Ireland following partition.[4] O'Neill's mother was often abroad and his aunt, Sylvia, did much to raise him.[5] Later, Terence O'Neill's colleagues would attribute his aloof and lonely manner to his lack of a father figure in youth.

O'Neill spent the first seven years of his life in London in the grand house of his liberal grandfather, Lord Crewe, run by ten servants including a nanny and a Swiss governess. Summer holidays were spent in Ulster, at the O'Neill residence of Shane's Castle.[6] This brought the young boy dangerously close to the IRA's campaign of arson against Ireland's 'Big Houses', targeted as political and potentially military bases of reaction against the Irish revolution. Ulster was not immune, though support for the Union there had a democratic basis extending far beyond the landed 'ascendancy'. In 1922, raiders arrived at Shane's Castle from Tyrone by boat in the dead of night. Lord O'Neill, in his eighty-third year, had to be carried from his home by stretcher. He wept as the flames consumed much of the mansion and its artistic treasures. It was believed by the family that the head forester on the estate, a catholic, had refused to raise the alarm. Lady O'Neill would often say to Terence, 'After all that kindness they burnt down my home.'[7]

Also in 1922, Terence's mother remarried to Hugh Dodds, the British consul in Addis Ababa. Terence's attitude towards him appears ambivalent. In his autobiography he never gave his name, introducing him only as 'a certain gentleman'. Still, when aged seven he travelled with his stepfather to Abyssinia it was 'undoubtedly the happiest year of my life.'[8] Here he lived in the faded grandeur of the ex-Imperial Russian Legation. An audience with the Regent, the future Emperor Haile Selassie, was organised for the young boy. Eating black bread and honey, the two chatted in

French. When velvet curtains were drawn back to introduce two lion cubs into the room, a startled Terence pulled his feet off the floor, and for this was slapped by his governess for behaving in an 'un-British' manner. Another time, whilst riding a pony and wearing a pith helmet, he was fired on by bandits who mistook his water jar for a weapon.[9]

O'Neill returned to England to attend school at West Downs in Winchester, then Eton.[10] To improve his French and acquire German, he spent 1936 in France and then Austria where he stayed with a determinedly anti-Nazi family. This experience turned him into a convinced opponent of appeasement back in Britain, a position which disturbed Lord Crewe and his family who were partisans of Neville Chamberlain.[11] 'I . . . tended to go the other way,' O'Neill recalled 'I always wanted to go into politics.'[12] Perhaps to curtail his political ambitions, in 1939 his aunt secured Terence a job as civilian *aide-de-camp* to the Governor of South Australia. Within a few weeks, however, war broke out and he returned to join the prestigious Irish Guards. In May 1940 he received his commission at Sandhurst and joined the Second Battalion of Irish Guards, known within the forces as 'The Micks'. Most of his fellow-soldiers were southern Irish, Liverpool Irish, or from Glasgow. Few were from Northern Ireland. In 1941 the Guards Armoured Division was formed. Whilst waiting for the invasion of Europe, Terence married Jean Whitaker. Jean, a devout Christian, had been born in 1915 to a wealthy and long established family owning the substantial Lisle Court estate near Lymington, Hampshire. Educated at home, Jean had developed impressively expert knowledge of gardening and horticulture. She was an out-doors sort who enjoyed sailing and who travelled by motorcycle to her war-work at the Royal Naval Hospital in Gospar. The wedding, on 4 February 1944, was in the Irish Guards chapel and the pair honeymooned at Cleggan Lodge, home of his aunt and uncle, in

Northern Ireland. They were met from the train by a horse-drawn jaunting cart.

Once in Europe O'Neill served as the Intelligence Officer of the 2nd battalion. He was noted by his fellow soldiers as 'the most tolerant of men and quite a Francophile'.[13] O'Neill was engaged in intense action and suffered tragedy, losing a good friend, David Peel, who had been his best man at his marriage, as well as both his brothers, the Hon. Brian O'Neill aged 29 with the 1st Battalion of the Irish Guards in Norway, 1940, and Lord (Shane) O'Neill aged 37 with the North Irish Horse in Italy in 1944. (Lord O'Neill's widow, Ann, went on to marry Lord Rothermere, owner of the *Daily Mail*, and then Ian Fleming, creator of James Bond).

Terence's was a particularly patrician war-experience. John Colville, O'Neill's cousin and Private Secretary to Churchill, remembers meeting O'Neill while on a brief tour of duty:

> He borrowed his Brigadier's jeep and together with an Australian brother officer of mine, we set off for the front line. We lunched off Camembert in a cornfield and then walked to Carpiquet airfield. . . . After being unceremoniously ejected when we ventured into Caen, of which our troops held only half . . . we all but stumbled into a minefield . . . Terence O'Neill, totally unperturbed, went into reverse and drove backwards to the Orne bridge singing, in his excellent tenor voice, '*Tout va Très Bien, Madame la Marquise*'.
>
> After this foolish escapade we went back to dine at Terence's Brigade Headquarters, disguising from the Brigadier how nearly we had lost both his jeep and his Intelligence Officer. Accustomed to the dull and repetitive 'compote' meals provided by the RAF, my Australian friend and I were astonished at the banquet Terence O'Neill offered us. In

addition to his other duties he was a catering officer with a flair and had imported, as a useful addition to more warlike equipment, a poultry farm. It had crossed the channel in the recesses of a LST (landing craft for tanks). The Brigade of Guards, as magnificent fighters as any in the world, saw no virtue in austerity on active service.[14]

The ease with which officers in the Irish Guards assumed superiority can be quite disconcerting to the modern reader:

The Brigade had taken a great many prisoners, including Russians conscripted by the Germans. Captain Terence O'Neill kept a pet Mongol youth for a week, to dig trenches and carry his kit and maps. The Mongol, when first ordered to dig, thought it was his grave and started to cry. Captain O'Neill explained, by mime and gesture, that it was for life, not death he was digging. The Mongol then kissed him and dug the snuggest slit-trench ever seen for his deliverer. After a week Divisional Headquarters ordered Captain O'Neill to give up his Mongol as a 'security measure'.[15]

By 10 September 1944 the Guards had fought their way to the Dutch frontier. They stayed for a week, and here O'Neill was injured, hit on the sciatic nerve by shrapnel when brigade headquarters came under artillery fire. As they were temporarily cut off, O'Neill was tended in a local house by the Ten Horn family, near Nijmegan in Holland. When O'Neill and his wife revisited in 1964, Mrs Ten Horn reminded Jean O'Neill: 'We had waited so long for liberation that nothing was too much. Your husband was forever apologising for troubling us.'[16] Captain O'Neill was evacuated back to England and the war came to a close before he could return to active service.

LIFE IN AHOGHILL

At the end of 1945 Terence and his family finally came to live in the north of Ireland, in a converted Regency rectory near Ahoghill, Glebe House. At the age of thirty-one the future Prime Minister of Northern Ireland for the first time settled down to live in the province. Previously he had never resided for more than a holiday season. The couple had one son, Patrick (b. 1945), and one daughter, Anne (b. 1947). Terence's wife, Jean, participated in community organisations such as the (exclusively protestant) Women's Guild and the local hunt. At home, the family had a home-help, dogs, cats and horses. Mrs O'Neill's garden had a particular reputation for magnificence, and Terence, though lacking his wife's knowledge and skill, cultivated his own arboretum.[17] O'Neill's hobbies – largely given up by the 1960s – included architecture, furniture, paintings, and antique collecting, particularly Victorian Staffordshire figurines.[18]

O'Neill's personal life, while no different in this respect from probably most unionist liberals, was almost hermetically sealed off from the catholic population. Ahoghill, where he had made his home, was divided even by Ulster standards, between Church of Ireland (O'Neill's church), Presbyterians, and Roman Catholics. Wits dubbed the village 'Ahoghill Les Trois Églises' after De Gaulle's rural retreat.[19] Notoriously, in the 1950s O'Neill placed an advertisement in a Belfast newspaper seeking a protestant house-maid. This, he explained unapologetically in 1972, was because on previous occasions there had been 'some trouble' over catholic staff, so they had 'advertised for a person of the protestant religion to stop catholics turning up'.[20] His daughter, Anne, born 1947, reminisced of her childhood in 1969:

I remember, as a kid, when I would talk to someone in the village. They might point out that so-and-so who is passing down the other side of the street is a catholic. We would just turn and stare. The impression was that they were something odd. Something to avoid, a lower class, segregated from the rest of us. And I remember the instructions I would get before I went riding – don't go through the village where there are rows of catholic houses. They might throw stones at you.

At the time of interview, Anne O'Neill had yet to meet any catholics, having gone to an English public school.[21]

THE NEW GENERATION

O'Neill was part of a unionist generation on the cusp of politics in Northern Ireland: notably Brian Faulkner (b. 1921), Bill Craig (b. 1924), and Ian Paisley (b. 1926). Faulkner, in contrast to O'Neill's gentry background, was quintessentially bourgeois, coming as he did from an ambitious family prominent in textiles, though his education near Dublin meant that he too had perspectives wider than that of insular Ulster. Faulkner's lack of military experience was to cost him dearly in the esteem of much of the Unionist establishment well into the 1960s, fuelling his resentment.[22] A military tradition carried an important kudos in Unionist politics. Terence O'Neill, it seems at the insistence of local politicians, retained his relatively low designation of 'Captain' until becoming a Lord in 1970.[23] It marked him out as one of a long line of aristocratic warriors who had served queen and country with savoir-faire and an upbeat combination of duty and adventure. Brian Faulkner, in contrast, always suffered for staying out of the armed forces during the War, to run his father's factory.

Bill Craig's war-career as a young RAF volunteer saw him serving bravely as a rear-gunner on a Lancaster Bomber: a notably dangerous posting, and perhaps formative of his future high-risk persona. He qualified as a solicitor shortly after the war, and was quickly perceived as representative of the forward-looking, professional middle-class, set against a Unionist establishment still dominated by industrial and landed elites. Craig made his way in the 1940s and 1950s though the professional dominated student and youth sections of the Unionist Party. Ian Paisley's background, in contrast, was plebeian, traditionally rural and religiously evangelical, and he early answered a calling to commit himself to the Christian ministry. Only 14 in 1940, he spent the latter war years as a student at the Reformed Presbyterian Church in Belfast. Before the war was out, he was invited to become a pastor in East Belfast.

A concerted nationalist campaign to delegitimise the border spearheaded by the all-Ireland Anti-Partition League meant that post-war politics in Northern Ireland pivoted as much as ever on the national question. The 1949 Stormont election – known as the 'Chapel Gate Election', because collections were taken outside Catholic churches throughout Ireland to finance anti-partition candidates – was a polarised referendum on the border, easily won by the Unionists. Northern Ireland's Stormont government, under Prime Minister Basil Brooke (Later Lord Brookeborough) was deeply traditionalist and fixated on the maintenance of partition. O'Neill was not particularly attracted to the Stormont cockpit, and tried to persuade his uncle, Lord Rathcavan, to secure him nomination for a vacant Westminster seat. The family still seemed opposed to Terence entering politics, however.[24] 'Circumstances decreed that I should stay at home,' O'Neill regretfully recalled.[25]

ULSTER POLITICS

The Ulster Unionist Party was officially allied to the British Conservative Party but, as a Tory guest of the Unionist Party from

Great Britain found, the dynamics of Ulster politics was quite distinct:

> Before I went to Ulster I was very ignorant about their problems and the general political climate existing in the Six Counties. . . . I discovered that the fundamental consideration in Ulster . . . was that the Unionist Party, neither in their local parliament at Stormont nor in what they term the 'Imperial' Parliament at Westminster, can risk losing a General election. . . . If the Nationalist Party were to win a majority at Stormont, they would undoubtedly elect immediately to federate Ulster with Eire; therefore the Unionist Party can never afford to lose. . . . This psychological attitude to domestic politics determines every action. The issue of partition is paramount. The fact that it is supported by protestants and opposed by catholics means that the political sentiment in Ulster is more pervasive and fundamental than in any other country in the world of which I have experience, except perhaps Greece.[26] The religious cleavage has, however, ensured that all political parties are more or less classless. It was very noticeable at the Ulster Unionist lunch that the representatives from the constituencies were entirely heterogeneous – Lords were sitting next to gamekeepers and Marquesses next to milk girls.[27]

This was the political arena in which O'Neill was fated to operate. In October 1946 the Stormont constituency of Bannside fell vacant. O'Neill secured the Ulster Unionist Party nomination and was returned unopposed in November 1946. His ability to finance himself was no doubt an important reason, along with his family reputation and war career, as to why O'Neill – as a relative outsider to Northern Ireland politics – was nominated by the local Unionist Association. As late as 1963, a Stormont MP earned £500 per annum less than a Junior Staff Officer.[28] Low salaries for MPs were consciously calculated to weaken parties such as the Northern

Ireland Labour Party (hereafter NILP), who lacked well-heeled candidates.[29] But it also helped to alienate the ambitious bourgeoisie. The lack of an able middle class in the Unionist Party was recognised by all sections of the party.[30]

O'Neill certainly found his fellow colleagues parochial and inward-looking. He remembered remarking to a fellow MP that Roman Catholics were only a very small minority in Great Britain, and being amused by the response: 'Boys a boys, Britain must be a wonderful protestant country.'[31] O'Neill only attempted to join his constituency Orange Lodge in 1952, and was rebuffed for the having had once remarked that 'he was as good a protestant out of the Institution as he would be were he in it'. Pressure from the Grand Master meant that he was admitted to a lodge in Ahoghill, but he was elected master only two years after becoming Prime Minister. No doubt he preferred his dual membership of the altogether more congenial elite Eldon lodge in Belfast.[32]

Bannside was one of seven County Antrim seats and was overwhelmingly rural. Despite a strong Liberal tradition, both O'Neill's Unionist predecessors had served until death, and O'Neill himself was returned unopposed in every election until 1969. Unsurprisingly, the Unionist associations in the area atrophied, and O'Neill was too focused on Stormont to help out much.

O'Neill made his maiden speech on the 1947 Education act. By introducing compulsory education to age fifteen, grammar-schools for those who passed the eleven-plus qualification exam, and increased state grants to Roman Catholic voluntary schools, this was later held to be seminal in the creation of a catholic-middle class who would seek civil rights in the late 1960s. At the time it cost the liberal minister Samuel Hall-Thompson his reputation with Unionist grassroots, and in 1954 he lost his seat to Norman Porter, secretary of the National Union of Protestants (of which Paisley was briefly a member).[33] In his memoirs, O'Neill called the 1947 education act Lord Brookeborough's 'last act of political courage'.[34]

Unionism was in a febrile state in the years succeeding the war. It was feared that the Labour Government in London might at worst show hostility to the Union with Northern Ireland, or at least force 'socialist measures' on the province. Some Unionists wondered whether Ulster's devolution government might not usefully be ramped up to 'dominion status', immune from British interference. In a 1947 speech to constituents, O'Neill argued in favour of Home Rule for Scotland (where Labour's election majority over the Conservatives in 1945 had been slight). This produced the headline in the local press, 'O'Neill in Favour of Scottish Nationalists'.[35] As it turned out, Labour was friendly to Northern Ireland's government. In 1949, in reaction to the declaration of the Irish Republic, Westminster passed the Ireland Act. This was seen as a great Unionist triumph, as it appeared to render the Union more secure by making its ending conditional on agreement from the Stormont parliament. On becoming Prime Minister, O'Neill would call the 1949 act Brookeborough's greatest achievement.[36] He clearly believed that, in copper-fastening partition, it allowed Unionism to move out of its defensive laager and engage more generously with the nationalist minority.

INTO GOVERNMENT

In February 1948 O'Neill was appointed Parliamentary Secretary to William Grant, Minister of Health, with special responsibility for housing. These eighteen months were described in a 1961 profile as O'Neill's most formative period.[37] Lacking any real apprenticeship in the ranks of the party or the Orange Order, O'Neill's association with Grant, an unusually working-class minister, was perhaps as close as he ever came to working with the plebeian base of Unionism. In 1954, O'Neill was required to shepherd the controversial Rent De-restriction Bill his new Minister, Dame Dehra Parker, was pushing through Stormont. This was considered by some a dangerous provocation of traditionally Unionist voting workers. The journalist John Cole, then with the *Belfast Telegraph*, thought that opposition to the bill heralded 'the first tremors of populism that has since produced Paisley . . . and the rest.'[38] O'Neill was adept at handling negotiations with his Westminster counterparts, but much less effective in winning over the Unionist Party. The Attorney General, Edmund Warnock, in 1956 spoke against the bill and resigned from the government.[39] In the resultant reshuffle Terence O'Neill, aged 42, finally reached Cabinet level as Minister of Home Affairs. Six months later he was appointed Minister of Finance.

O'Neill's relatively long delay in reaching the Cabinet was not due to lack of ability or application. He recalled later:

I do remember when I was asked to join the Cabinet my predecessor saying to me: 'There'll be absolutely nothing to do, you know . . . half an hour in the office once a week will be plenty'. And I said to him: 'Please don't worry about that. If I take the job on I'm going to do it properly.' And he looked really rather surprised that I should want to.[40]

O'Neill was virtually unique in the cabinet in having no outside business interests, nor any need to supplement his meagre ministerial salary. His work ethic was a novelty in Stormont circles. In 1964 he told an interviewer that, on average he worked 15 or 16 hours a day:

I think that these days any Prime Minister – and indeed any Cabinet Minister – must expect to have to reduce his personal and private commitments to a minimum. If he is putting private inclinations before his public duties he is not doing his job properly. This may sound a rather austere way to live, but it is, I believe, necessary in these modern times. The days of the amateur, part-time man in public life are a thing of the past.[41]

This attitude derived, in nearly equal measure, from O'Neill's sense of almost military duty and a right to lead, and his personal inclination born of a certain shyness. When under strain, as he often was during his premiership, the former dominated. In January 1969 he spoke wistfully of the responsibilities honour demanded: 'I have no intention of resigning. After six years in a job like this you don't just lay down your burden and walk out. You feel you must soldier on.'[42]

But, in truth, O'Neill's passion was for politics. Even when retired he filled his available hours by

read[ing] newspapers, all day almost, and biographies, particularly of politicians. I don't have much time for music. I used to like some stuff in the '30s, jazz and a bit of Carol Gibbons, but I don't bother now one way or another. . . . I used to ride a lot, but it went out of my life a long time ago, as did shooting game. And I never had the patience to fish. I've never been to Croke Park in my life.'[43]

Here was a meticulous, efficient and conscientious politician, but not a relaxed party 'boss', easy with small talk, idle socialising and patronage. The contrast with the shooting, fishing, genial and popular Brookeborough, or Faulkner who made friends with even the likes of Charles Haughey and Seán Lemass through a common enthusiasm for fox-hunting, is striking.

O'Neill did not get on with the permanent secretary at the Ministry of Finance, Douglas Harkness, who was close to Brookeborough and sceptical of activism in devolved government.[44] Rather than work through Harkness, he cultivated direct relations with British and Northern Ireland civil servants.[45] A 1961 profile noted that 'when presented with a file requiring a decision, he . . . likes to pursue the problem back through the various civil servants who have contributed to it – and seldom discusses an issue with his senior officials until he has gone through the process of research.'[46] In April 1962 he jocularly commented that 'I hope I don't appear frivolous in saying that what I most enjoy is arguing things out with my civil servants.'[47] His closest aides were Ken Bloomfield, his speech-writer, Jim Malley, his Private Secretary, and Cecil Bateman, Secretary to the Cabinet.[48]

O'Neill's enthusiasm for technical fixes could see him quite lose touch with the politics of the possible. In 1958, for example, he circulated cabinet colleagues with a plan to deal with chronically high unemployment:

> All ideas should be considered. . . . For good measure I will put one up to be shot down – perhaps with some scorn and derision. Can Lough Neagh be drained? It would be equivalent to a new county. Have engineers – possibly Dutch engineers – ever been consulted? The Government could possibly lease it out in 100-acre farms. County Neagh would have no mountains or bogs and might be quite fertile, it could be planted with trees and people and a new town could be built at its centre. (Strangford is smaller and has salt water and tide but could perhaps also be considered.)[49]

There was always something of the dreamer about O'Neill.

David Gordon has argued that O'Neill's evident enthusiasm for devolution was dangerous, in that it celebrated a little-Ulsterism, inevitably focussed on the national question, as preferable to the pragmatic politics of economic and social development typical of sovereign states such as Great Britain (or southern Ireland). This, Gordon argues counter-intuitively, was to make O'Neill 'the most reactionary of all the Unionist Prime Ministers.'[50] O'Neill instinctive internationalism, however, gave him a realistic view of Northern Ireland's true stature. Stormont, he thought, was equivalent to 'a State Parliament in Australia or a Provincial Parliament in Canada.'[51] O'Neill obviously had a considerable interest in and respect for countries which had achieved more rational forms of devolution that the pseudo-sovereign pretensions of Northern Ireland with its grandiloquent parliament buildings and affectation of a fully-fledged cabinet government. Interestingly, O'Neill was to describe himself as a 'Progressive Conservative in the Canadian sense.'[52] Perhaps he identified with John Diefenbaker, the contemporary liberal-Tory and royalist leader of Scottish-German descent who championed the 'non-hypothecated Canadian' against the divisive claims of Canadian-English and Canadian-French. O'Neill, similarly, presumed to speak for the striving but apolitical Ulster citizen.

O'Neill was certainly influenced by the writings of Samuel Smiles, a Victorian ex-radical who had found fame (after writing a history of Ireland) with his bestseller, *Self-Help, with Illustrations of Character and Conduct* (1859). This promoted the virtue of entrepreneurial individualism both on economic and moral grounds. O'Neill as Finance Minister developed a distinctive public message, urging his fellow citizens to cultivate the virtues of 'self-help' rather than rely on hand-outs:

> [T]he Ulsterman of today has perhaps a special aptitude for making out a special case for special treatment. . . . Edwardian Ulster was the Ulster of self-reliance and Elizabethan Ulster has become the Ulster of state assistance and state security. We need all our native wit and

thrift and common sense during the days that lie ahead to ensure a prosperous and happy future for our children and grandchildren.[53]

O'Neill presented himself as an almost apolitical voice of reason. He avoided both excesses of traditionalism and dangerous liberalism. When a controversy blew up in 1959 on whether the Unionist Party should accept catholics as members, O'Neill held aloof, simply calling for party unity.[54]

Faulkner, in contrast, threw himself into modernising the Ulster Unionists, and was a dynamic force in the Unionist Society – the closest thing to a party 'think-tank' – and the Young Unionist Movement. He wished to make the party more accessible to the professional middle class in particular. Faulkner had been invited to stand in the notoriously divisive 1949 'Chapel Gate election' by O'Neill himself.[55] But as an MP in the 1950s, Faulkner's focus shifted to the Orange Order, a body bringing all classes of protestant together. He became Minister of Home Affairs in 1959 (a post O'Neill had briefly held), and in this post gained some notoriety as a defender of Northern Ireland's segregated and discriminatory order. He was best known for introducing internment against the IRA's 'Border Campaign' (1956–62) and rationalising – whilst maintaining intact – the legal basis of gerrymandered electoralism (by which constituency lines were drawn to over-represent protes-tants, especially in local government) with the 1962 Electoral Law Bill. William Craig was initially very much a protégé of Faulkner, succeeding him as chairman of the Young Unionist Society, and upon election to Stormont consciously positioning himself as a voice of the rising generation of middle class Unionism. Once in Stormont, however, he gravitated towards O'Neill's technocratic brand of modernisation. Paisley, for his part, was on the margins. He had set up his own free Presbyterian Church in 1951 and attached himself to the working-class and plebeian hard-line wing of the Ulster Unionist Party, before breaking away from the party in protest at its rhetorical distancing from embattled sectarian militancy and its embrace of devolutionist complacency. Already, O'Neill represented the smooth kind of Unionism Paisley despised.

CHAPTER 2

Into the Premiership

Politics in the late 1950s and early 1960s was dominated not by community relations but by the weak state of the economy. Agricultural under-employment was widespread. The region suffered from a range of natural disadvantages – a small population, a lack of resources (coal, minerals and so on), and the added burden of cross-channel transport costs on imports and exports.[1] Conservatively managed family firms dominated the local economy, and – despite O'Neill's Smilesian strictures – Northern Ireland property owners proved to be poor entrepreneurs.[2] Well-paid employment in traditional industry – aircraft production, shipbuilding and linen manufacture – was in decline.[3] The rise of German and Japanese shipyards and slowness of management to modernise, especially to shift from riveting to welding techniques, all served to undermine Harland and Wolff Shipyard's pre-eminence.[4] The ocean liner *Canberra*, launched in March 1960, was the last of a long line of Belfast built liners.[5] By the end of the 1958, 40,000 were on the dole – 8.3 per cent of the insured workforce.

THE CRISIS OF UNIONIST ECONOMIC STRATEGY

There was a general resistance in London political circles to allowing Northern Ireland special help solely due to its unemployment

problem, for fear that depressed regions in Great Britain would
look for something similar. However, the province's peculiar
political and security problems for some time exercised a decisive
influence. The Secretary of State at the Home Office, in a memorandum to the cabinet, wrote in 1955 that:

> The Union creates particularly tiresome problems for the Government
> of the United Kingdom . . . Nevertheless it must be recognised that
> the possession of Northern Ireland is of capital importance to the
> defence of Great Britain. . . . If we desire to retain Northern Ireland . . .
> it is most important politically to be able to demonstrate that Northern
> Ireland benefits from the Union.[6]

The Home Secretary concurred that 'a high level of unemployment where there is a large and potentially violent dissident minority
may easily lead to serious civil disorders.'[7] As a result, the principle
of 'leeway', in addition to that of parity of taxation and social
services, was agreed by Whitehall in 1955.[8] 'Leeway' allowed what
Arthur Green, Assistant Secretary in the Department of Finance,
called an 'expenditure based system' in which the British 'subven-
tion' would be determined not by a fixed scheme formula but on a
case by case basis.[9] Though the Treasury could veto any single project
outside the principle of parity costing over £50,000, Westminster
exercised virtually no scrutiny, it being left in the main to civil
servants.[10]

Ironically, Stormont's success in limiting the IRA Border
Campaign (1956–62), and the failure of catholics to offer it militant
support, undermined British fears that Northern Ireland's economic
lag might be politically problematic. In contrast to the mid-1950s,
when the principle of leeway had been conceded, by the 1960s
Great Britain was much less concerned that high unemployment
in Northern Ireland would create sectarian disorder or a catholic

uprising.[11] Westminster, therefore, refused any substantial response to Brookeborough's 1960 plea for further economic succour.[12]

Labour in Northern Ireland saw its chance. Since the early 1950s, the NILP had reconstituted itself as a social democratic party. It was in favour of partition but insisted that Irish nationalism no longer threatened the Union with Great Britain. In criticising the dominant parties as reactionary 'Orange and Green Tories', the NILP was attempting to make itself the true party of post-war British modernity. The party focussed its attacks on the Unionist Party as a bulwark of archaic gentry-rule reliant on populist scaremongering. A swing of 6 per cent towards NILP had netted it four marginal Belfast seats in the 1958 Stormont general election: David Bleakley in Victoria, Tom Boyd in Pottinger, William Boyd in Woodvale and Vivian Simpson in Oldpark. All four MPs were well-known for their protestant faith as well as their labour politics. Woodvale and Victoria were solidly proletarian and protestant constituencies, while Oldpark and Pottinger had substantial catholic votes. Together they raised the prospect of an erosion of Unionist support amongst urban workers, and an alliance of convenience between disaffected protestants and incorrigibly oppositionist catholics.

THE POTTINGER SPEECH

The NILP was clearly seen by the Unionist Party as a potentially dynamic force. Already in 1958, O'Neill had been cited in a *New Statesman* article as saying that he expected their parliamentary representation to double at the next general election.[13] The Unionists were increasingly concerned. Might they be displaced at Stormont by a nationalist-labour alliance? It was a still distant but increasingly plausible possibility. When the next general election came around in May 1962, the NILP won no new seats, but its vote reached 26 per cent, 16 per cent higher than in 1958. Alone they nearly equalled the Unionist vote of 67,450 in Belfast, winning 60,170; the 5,049 business votes in the Belfast seats, which presumably went overwhelming Unionist, nearly made up the difference.

Something had to be done to restore the Unionist reputation for competence. In May 1961 the British and Stormont governments had established a joint working party on Northern Ireland's economy. It was chaired by Sir Robert Hall, a high-powered economist who had coordinated economic advice for the British Government until April that year.[14] Hall, however, saw himself as representing the interests of the British Treasury. Proposals from the Northern Ireland side to subsidise employment were shot down.[15] The report was finally published in October 1962, during the Cuban Missile Crisis.[16] Dismally, it advised that 'steps . . . be taken to find employment opportunities outside Northern Ireland and to induce unemployed workers to avail themselves of them.'[17] This case for emigration from Ulster was particularly unwelcome for unionists who were already fearful of protestants leaving a sinking-ship.[18] Brookeborough dismissed its recommendations nearly out of hand. He feared that economic stagnation – unemployment still ran at 8 per cent and rising – made the NILP 'the enemy at the gate'.[19]

Paul Bew, Peter Gibbon and Henry Patterson, in their classic study, capture very well the pressure the NILP placed upon Unionism.[20] Of course, crisis for Unionism did not predetermine who would succeed Brookeborough. It was O'Neill who grabbed the moment to articulate a positive Unionist response to the Hall Report. He did this on 29 November 1962 in what became known as the 'Pottinger Speech'.[21] When anthologised in 1969, the speech was highlighted at foundational to his premiership: 'It is not often that a Prime Minister . . . can look back on a single speech as setting a keynote for his administration. It is rarer still that such a speech provided in itself much of the impetus for his elevation to the premiership. These comments can, however, be fairly made of . . . the "Pottinger Speech".'[22] O'Neill addressed a Unionist Association in what was no doubt deliberately chosen as an NILP-held constituency. He argued for investment in Northern Ireland not simply to shore up declining industries, but as part of a United Kingdom modernisation. It was in Great Britain's interest to direct resources to the province as part of its effort to take the pressure off an over-heating south-east England. Northern Ireland should be catching-up with Great Britain, developing new cutting-edge industries, not just keeping pace. Rather than seeking to subsidise the traditional (and protestant) heavy industries, O'Neill proposed radically re-shaping the infrastructure of Northern Ireland to accommodate new investment projects.

The Pottinger Speech was an innovation in Unionist political discourse, but it amplified pre-existing noises from the Northern Ireland civil service. Anxious to exploit the potential opened by the 'lee-way' principle, the civil servants were already busy cooking up plans.[23] In 1960, Sir Robert Matthew had been asked to draw up a 'development plan' for the Greater Belfast region.[24] Published on 26 February 1963, Matthew's report proposed a huge plan of investment, especially in the creation of a 'new city' between Lurgan and Portadown, the designation of a series of growth points, and an expanded motorway and road network.[25] The idea was that while Britain would not invest simply to shore up traditional protestant industrial employment , it would finance bold new initiatives to modernise and attract private investment. O'Neill's 'Pottinger Speech' articulated this new strategy, and set O'Neill up for the succession.

TO THE PREMIERSHIP

In March 1963 Brookeborough, aged 74, was admitted to hospital
for eleven days to have a duodenal ulcer and a hernia treated. On 23
March Lord Wakehurst, the province's Crown representative, was
summoned by Lady Brookeborough. Upon his arrival Brookeborough announced that he was resigning due to ill health.[26] A
discussion was held on the possible successor. Wakehurst later
recorded that he and Lord Brookeborough 'were of one mind in
considering the Minister of Finance and acting Prime Minister,
Captain Terence O'Neill, as the obvious choice.' O'Neill, he
believed, had emerged as the front runner since the 'Pottinger
Speech'. Brookeborough, however, refused to publicly name a
successor. From Terence O'Neill's account, Lady Brookeborough
seems to have dominated her husband's itinerary and business during
his convalescence,[27] and it may be that she pressed Brookeborough
not to recommend his real favourite, Brian Faulkner, who she considered something of an upstart and whose able wife she resented.[28]

O'Neill was called to Governor Wakehurst's house at 6 pm the
following Monday, the 25th. Following an interview with Lord
Brookeborough, O'Neill consulted with Bill Craig, only elected to
Stormont (for Larne) in 1960, but in a Parliamentary Party not
overburdened with talent, already he was the Unionist chief whip.[29]
Craig's soundings of Unionist MPs in the Stormont Commons
found sixteen favouring O'Neill and nine each for Brian Faulkner
and John Andrews.[30] Craig, thus, helped O'Neill into the Premier-
ship, blocking a frustrated Faulkner. O'Neill's elevation was
controversial from the start because, as Wakehurst recorded, the
Unionist Party felt aggrieved at not being formally consulted.[31] In
October 1963, Edmund Warnock circulated a letter to fellows
Unionist MPs. He protested that the Cabinet, the Parliamentary
Party, and the Ulster Unionist Council had been 'completely

ignored.'[32] Nothing came of the letter, but it showed clearly enough that O'Neil's right to rule was questioned from the outset.

Faulkner, hobbled by his lack of military service, identification with lambeg-bashing unionism, and the personal animosity of Lady Brookeborough, felt cheated. The 'fur coat' brigade, he believed, had promoted one of their own. It was impossible to exclude Faulkner from the cabinet, but from here on he was to wage a tenacious and destructive guerrilla campaign against Prime Minister O'Neill, whilst simultaneously burnishing his reputation as an exceptionally able and hard-working Minister of Commerce.

O'Neill became Prime Minister aged 48, after 17 years in political office. He saw himself as one of a new generation of leaders, identifying strongly with his contemporaries, US President John F. Kennedy and Canadian Prime Minister Lester B. Pearson. In April 1963, shortly after becoming Prime Minister, O'Neill invited President Kennedy, who was already scheduled to visit the Irish republic, to come north and open the recently re-furbished Giant's Causeway.[33] Kennedy declined, perhaps agreeing with Samuel Johnson that the Giant's Causeway is 'worth seeing . . . but not worth going to see.'[34] Northern Ireland was only represented in the official reception by Nationalist Party MPs. Kennedy's comment in his speech to the Dáil – 'Free Ireland will not be satisfied with anything less than liberty' – was taken to be a veiled condemnation of partition and apparently replaced more direct references excised at the eleventh hour.[35] Even after Kennedy's assassination in November 1963, grass-roots Unionist opinion remained bitter. Belfast Corporation refused to approve 'John F. Kennedy' as a name for the new road through Turf Lodge and petitions were raised in Carrickfergus against a proposed 'Kennedy Drive' on the grounds that the President had 'insulted' Northern Ireland in turning down O'Neill's invitation.[36] O'Neill, in contrast, gladly kept a picture of JFK and Jackie over his fireplace.[37]

In his encounters with America, however, O'Neill brought rather traditional Ulster (and British upper-class) sensibilities. In September 1963 and March 1964 he visited North America. In a 1963 diary, he recorded with satisfaction a talk with Pierson Dixon, in the British Consulate in New York:

> He said that the Chinese Ambassador the other day had suggested to him that the reason why both America and Canada had succeeded was because of their protestant influence and the reason why South America had failed was because of its catholic influence. *Tiens!*[38]

Still, regardless of the presumed 'burden' of the catholic minority in Northern Ireland, O'Neill was committed to a domestic modernisation project, based up catching up the 'lee-way' with Great Britain by furnishing an infrastructure capable of attracting private investment. British support for this was by no means assured.[39] O'Neill had to make the case, and in so doing he deployed the rhetoric of community cohesion and self-help.

TRANSFORMING THE FACE OF ULSTER

Speaking in Cardiff in March 1964, O'Neill told a sympathetic Welsh audience that 'the so called provinces really matter. Much of the inventive genius, the manufacturing skill and the sheer vigour of Britain is located here. I believe that great dividends await the Government – of whatever complexion – which can really put the under-used resources of areas remote from London to work.'[40] O'Neill believed that Northern Ireland was uniquely placed to benefit from such regional planning. This was the theme of his speech to the 1964 Lord Mayor's show in Belfast: 'We have a head start in all this activity. Ours is a closely knit community with its own Parliament and its own distinctive and well established machinery of government. We have the tools already to hand; let us therefore finish the job.'[41] He later predicted that, 'using means closely attuned to our own particular needs', Northern Ireland would achieve economic and social parity with Britain within forty years.[42]

O'Neill looked to physical planning as a means by which renew the province's attractiveness to investors. He explained this when reopening the Giant's Causeway in June 1963:

> The businessman who visits our Ministry of Commerce to discuss setting up a new industry may well have to live here himself. It follows that he examines not only our labour supply, our transport services and industrial grants, but the whole environment in which he is to live. We must, therefore, have a great deal more positive planning in Ulster before ribbon development and urban sprawl stealthily rob us of our birthright.[43]

In his first major speech as Prime Minister, to the Annual Meeting of the Ulster Unionist Council on 5 April 1963, and with the British Home Secretary Henry Brooke in the audience, he was messianic: 'Our task is to literally transform the face of Ulster.'[44] O'Neill was speaking quite literally, of physical and environmental transformation. But he also had in mind a wider project, which was later to develop very significantly, of civic engagement:

> We must become a participating rather than a spectator society. . . . Able people will serve the State, whether at party, political or administrative level, only if they believe that they will be able to make some real contribution to the life of Ulster, some real impact upon its major problems.[45]

This prefigured important features of O'Neillism: his desire to involve those of the middle classes in particular who held aloof from the traditional Unionist establishment, and to build a state that could claim the loyalty of all, including, implicitly, the currently alienated catholics. For now, however, economic modernisation was to the forefront. The shift from a regional economy based upon heavy industry to one hoping to utilise cutting-edge entrepreneurial energies required a commensurate higher-educational system. In November 1963 the government established a committee, headed by Sir John Lockwood, to make the case for a second university.

O'Neill promoted his protégé Bill Craig to Minister for Development, tasked with developing nothing less than a province-wide integrated 'lineal city', united by a new motorway, made up of Dungannon, Coleraine, Ballymena, Antrim, and Belfast.[46] A massive road building plan was to replace much of the rail network.[47] Professor Thomas Wilson, Adam Smith Chair of Political Economy at Glasgow University was commissioned to draw up an Economic Plan for the province.[48] The Cabinet supported the initiative because not only was 'Professor Wilson an able economist, but he was the most suitable on constitutional and political grounds.'[49] (Wilson was indeed quite reliable from a Unionist point of view: he refused to meet a Nationalist deputation to discuss discrimination).[50] Wilson's Economic Plan was announced by O'Neill in Parliament on 23 October 1963. It was an effective tilt against the NILP that had long been promoting planning. As the *News Letter* put it:

> The Government's wholehearted acceptance of the principle of economic planning was greeted with ironical Labour cheers, but Captain O'Neill pointed out quickly it was the Liberal Party and not the Conservatives who had a laissez faire policy. Nevertheless, there were feelings among the Labour members yesterday that the Government had stolen their thunder.[51]

O'Neill was quite content to take credit for this stroke, and quoted the 'stolen thunder' phrase in his autobiography.[52]

Planning meant co-operation with the trade unions. This raised the problem of the trade unions' Northern Ireland Committee (NIC) which was not recognised by Stormont because, as Unionist MP Edmund Warnock put it 'the Irish Congress of Trade Unions is a body completely dominated by ardent Republicans, and . . . is opposed to the very existence of a Northern Ireland Government or State.'[53] Quick progress was held up by Faulkner's grudging attitude, and Craig's modernising contempt for the 'restrictive practices' of trade unions.[54] Only on 30 June 1964 did a seventy-five minute meeting of the Parliamentary Unionist Party approve recognition of the NIC. In 1965, O'Neill could look back on his preparatory reforms with some satisfaction:

> We have the blueprints; we have the machinery to implement them both inside and outside the Government. We now face the long, difficult, arduous but immensely worthwhile task of turning plans into realities, of converting programmes into brick and mortar. . . . We must keep on with the task of modernising Ulster.[55]

O'Neill's ability to talk as a modernising, technocratic moderate in British circles worked wonders. He was justifiably proud in looking back:

> We had motorways in Northern Ireland before they existed in Scotland; and when the Treasury tried to stop our motorway programme I appealed to Lord Home, who was then Prime Minister – in fact I came over and saw him in the Cabinet Room – and despite the fact that he had by then become a Scottish Member of Parliament and knew that Scotland had no motorways, he allowed us to continue with our programme. So do not be misled by what happened in Northern

Ireland. Northern Ireland has been ruined not by its administrative set up but, I fear, by bigotry.[56]

Modernisation programmes could not, however, be easily differentiated from 'bigotry'. On a visit to the United States in 1963, O'Neill visited a museum 'and saw the plans for a new Philadelphia. New vistas – the mall in front of Independence Hall entailing wholesale demolition. New blocks for business purposes. Removal of slums. Could a dictatorship do more? Could Belfast do a sixteenth of this without a riot?'[57] He was right to be concerned that controversy must dog modernisation in Northern Ireland.

The centrepiece of the Matthew Plan was nothing less than a new city, to be developed between, and eventually incorporating, Lurgan and Portadown. On 9 December 1964 a detailed plan and report on the New City was published. It was to be a 'motor-car city' with a modern and efficient infrastructure covering 6,000 acres, and have a population of 100,000 by 1981.[58] The New City needed a name. An early runner was 'Knockmena', a corruption of the townland name Knockmenagh. George Clark, Grand Master of the Orange Order, proposed 'Clanrolla' or 'Lisnaminty', both local Irish names.[59] These were rejected by the chief planning officer, James Aitken: 'We must have a name that can be pronounced equally easily in all the capitals of the world, from New York and Hong Kong to Berlin. That would seem to rule out any of the more ornate Irish suggestions, anyway.'[60] Led by Faulkner and Craig, the cabinet settled on 'Craigavon', perhaps less than euphonious but a tribute to the Unionist hero and first Prime Minister of Northern Ireland. On the back-foot, O'Neill warned his colleagues that such a name would 'divide the community'.[61] So it did. In Stormont, the Nationalist MP, Joseph Connellan, heckled Craig's announcement of the name with: 'A protestant city for a protestant people.'[62] The *Belfast Telegraph* thought the name 'incredibly bad'.[63]

On 13 May 1964, O'Neill met with the Parliamentary Unionist party to discuss the New City. Using figures supplied by the Registrar General's office, he pointed out that catholics migrating in search of work from counties Down and Fermanagh were putting Unionists seats at risk in County Armagh. The unionist majority had fallen by 5000 over twelve years. A New City, he argued, would right the balance by retaining and attracting protestants. Unionist local authorities, he reassured the party, would ensure that only a limited number of houses would be allocated to catholics.[64] Geoffrey Copcutt, head of the design team working on the 'New City', got wind of the conspiracy and resigned: 'Religious and political considerations are dominant in the New City area . . . a sinister springboard is being sought.'[65]

Craigavon was indeed designed to be a 'sinister springboard' gathering protestants by 'selective intake' from greater Belfast, so as to push unionist electoral hegemony further west. While the first report on the New City, written by Copcutt, had made it clear that most of the projected new population was supposed to come from the predominantly catholic south and west of Northern Ireland, where unemployment was high, in the second report, after his resignation, it was explicitly stated that new residents would be funnelled from Belfast so that 'the proportions of families in the different community groupings will be similar to that of the Province as a whole.'[66] This of course, would mean a protestant majority: a gerrymandered city as a *synecdoche* of the statelet. Consequently, grants were explicitly targeted on migrants from Belfast. (Ironically, once the Troubles erupted, most of these turned out to be catholic refugees from the capital.)[67]

The Second University roused even more of a storm. On 10 February 1965 the Lockwood Committee recommended that it be sited not in Londonderry, the front-runner in the public mind, but in the small protestant town of Coleraine on the north coast.[68] As a gratuitous snub, Derry was not even nominated for an entirely speculative third university. Derry, a majority nationalist city long resentful at living under a gerrymandered Unionist council, was stirred to action and a University for Derry action committee announced a city-wide general strike in the city and a motorcade from Derry to Stormont.[69] To avoid strike action, the Unionist controlled city council declared the day of action a public holiday.[70] They even participated in the motorcade, Lord Mayor Albert Anderson sharing a car with local Nationalist MP, Eddie McAteer.[71] Official Unionist solidarity was a sham, however. Rumours of local Unionist connivance in Derry's betrayal were soon abroad. In May Dr Robert Nixon, a Unionist MP, addressed Londonderry Middle Liberties Young Unionist association. 'There are Unionists who see Derry as a Papist city and say that it must be allowed to run down', he alleged, accusing 'nameless, faceless men from Londonderry'.[72]

On 27 May the Nationalist MP Patrick Gormley named these seven 'faceless men' in Stormont. They were: Gerald S. Glover (president of the City of Derry and Foyle Unionist Association and ex-Lord Mayor), Rev. John Brown, Rev. Professor R. L. Marshall, Mr J. F. Bond (a 'solicitor to the Unionist Party'), Dr Abernathy (head of the Apprentice Boys of Derry), Robert Stewart (a businessman), and Sidney Buchanan (a journalist and BBC correspondent in Derry).[73] Nixon reported, after meeting with O'Neill, that 'the Prime Minister himself told us that leading Unionist citizens in Derry were against new industries and the new university coming to Derry, and indeed that the siting of Coolekeeragh power station there was against their advice and wishes.'[74] It is no surprise that civil rights agitation was to detonate in Derry.

Despite these controversies, O'Neill modernisation, at least as a political stroke, had some success. When O'Neill called a general election in November 1965, it was with the aim of rolling back the

NILP in Belfast: 'You have only to look at the trend for the last fifteen years to see that the Unionists will have to fight their own corner in the city.'[75] Turn-out was poor, but while the Unionist vote fell, that of the NILP fell further, and they lost two of their four seats. The fifteen-year trend was reversed. This bolstered O'Neill in the short-run, but deprived Stormont of progressive voices sympathetic to his bridge-building.

Overall, O'Neill's attempt to 'Transform the Face of Ulster' must be considered a failure. The road building programme contributed to the disruption of settled communities, and in time some projects were cancelled.[76] The New City fell far short of its population target, reaching only 57,000 by 1980.[77] Craigavon never became a real city, local services were poor, and council politics were wracked with bitter sectarian division.[78] Until July 1966, it is true, unemployment in Northern Ireland was on a downward trend. New inward investment was pulled into O'Neill's 'transformed' Ulster, from Rolls Royce, Goodyear, Michelin, and Hoechst, for which hard-working Minister of Commerce Brian Faulkner got much credit. But when a UK credit squeeze was imposed the problem of lack of manufacturing jobs re-emerged.[79] A crisis at the Queen's Shipyard in 1966 forced the government to support Harland and Wolff at cost of £5 million. It was back to government bailouts for traditional employers, a kind of 'soup kitchen', as Prime Minister Harold Wilson sardonically rebuked O'Neill in 1968.[80]

Though hardly a shining example of 'self-help', what O'Neill certainly did achieve was a fundamental shift in the financial relationship with Britain. Public spending per head for the first time out-stripped that in England, though it still lagged behind that in Wales and especially Scotland.[81] For Unionism, O'Neill's success in extracting funds from Britain proved to be a poisoned chalice. It forced Stormont to adopt a policy of 'modernisation' that soon raised the question of when this would apply to civil rights anomalies such as discrimination in jobs and public housing, the gerrymandering of constituencies, and the limited rate-payers franchise in local government elections. As Britain would eventually make very clear, if Northern Ireland failed to deal with these problems, the faucet of discretionary funding could easily be turned off again.

CHAPTER 3

O'Neillism and Paisleyism

Northern Ireland's official culture was deeply antithetical to expressions of Irish nationalism. In 1954, the Stormont government had passed the Flags and Emblems Act. This had effectively criminalised the Irish tri-colour flag, as it had to be removed from display should anyone complain. Though deeply illiberal, the measure was not controversial even with moderate unionists. Denis Barritt and Charles Carter, both Quakers and so somewhat tangential to the established Orange/Green divide, had on behalf of the Irish Association conducted a path-breaking survey of community relations from 1959. It was eventually published in October 1962 as *The Northern Ireland Problem*, after being serialised in nine parts by an enthusiastic *Belfast Telegraph*.[1] Discussing the Flags and Emblems Act they expressed the opinion that 'it would in our view be unreasonable to expect a Unionist government to treat expressions of loyalty and of disloyalty with the even-handed 'justice' which is demanded of Nationalist opinion.'[2] Irish nationalists, however, resisted their marginalisation. In June 1963 the RUC had mobilised to prevent a tricolour being carried to Casement Park by republicans commemorating Wolfe Tone's centenary.[3] A tricolour was successfully and peacefully flown by a march to Milltown cemetery on the anniversary of the 1916 Easter Rising in 1964.[4]

BRIDGE-BUILDING

It was the matter of the Union flag that had first raised Ian Paisley to political prominence as an inveterate opponent of O'Neill's building bridges policy. In 1963 he had protested against the flying of the Union flag at half-mast over Belfast city hall to commiserate on the death of the pope. Paisley again made the front pages when republican flags sparked riots in the Westminster General Election of September 1964. These took place in the West Belfast constituency, particularly fraught as after boundary changes it was moving from Unionist to nationalist representation. At first the unfurling of the tricolour and the starry plough over the Republican election headquarters on Divis Street, off the Falls Road, had gone unremarked. Once it attracted Paisley's attention, however, protests flooded in to the police.[5] The Unionist candidate for West Belfast, James Kilfedder, sent a telegram to the Minister of Home Affairs: 'Remove tricolour in Divis Street which is aimed to provoke and insult loyalists in West Belfast.'[6] Twice, the RUC broke into the Republican offices with pickaxes and crowbars to tear down the offending flags.[7] On the second occasion, a crowd of some hundreds gathered, singing rebel songs, and a pitched-battle with police developed. It turned into the worst night of rioting for thirty years.[8] In response O'Neill one-sidedly attacked the republicans, but he also highlighted the twin aims of his administration so far – to advance Northern Ireland economically, and 'to build bridges between the two traditions within the community.' So, for the first time and in rather inauspicious circumstances, O'Neill introduced his 'bridge-building' slogan.[9]

More positively, on 24 April 1964 O'Neill had visited Lady of Lourdes Intermediate School, where he watched a hurling match – a Gaelic game never before countenanced by a Unionist politician – between Dunloy and Loughguile teams.[10] In the summer of 1965,

Jean O'Neill opened the carefully tended family garden to visitors. One visitor was the wife of the Lady of Lourdes' principal. She asked for, and was given, a plant for the school's garden, as a memento of O'Neill's historic visit.[11]

Much more dramatic was O'Neill's summit with Seán Lemass, the Taoiseach (Prime Minister) of Ireland. There was no reason in principle why the premiers of Ireland north and south could not meet. Lord Brookeborough claimed that such a meeting had been considered while he was premier, but ruled out due to the IRA campaign.[12] Nonetheless, as one put it in 1964, Unionists feared that such a meeting would be seen as 'a sort of latter day Niall of the Nine Hostages coming to pay homage to the High King of Ireland'.[13] Indeed, for some eighteen months before the summit, there had been a kind of megaphone diplomacy, as Lemass made speeches suggesting reconciliation and O'Neill responded with tart defences of Northern Ireland's constitutional status.

In late 1965, Brian Faulkner offered ministerial talks with his ministerial opposite number, Jack Lynch.[14] This finally propelled O'Neill into action.[15] But even though the timing of the summit came as a surprise, and seemed to contradict O'Neill's publicly wary response to Lemass, there's no doubt that he personally was enthusiastic about cross-border rapprochement. In political society at large the surprise was not the meeting, but its timing. As Eddie McAteer, Nationalist leader, commented 'the inevitable has happened a few months earlier than expected.'[16]

O'Neill failed to inform his Cabinet colleagues in advance of the meeting, despite the urgings of his Cabinet Secretary, Cecil Bateman.[17] O'Neill seems to have taken some relish in the cloak and dagger orchestration of the summit; he called it 'a real James Bond type operation.'[18] But he was mostly concerned, not unreasonably, that some of his cabinet colleagues would seek to sabotage the meeting if they had advance notice. 'If there had been a leak,' he recalled, 'we would have had trees felled by the IRA all along the road from Dublin to Belfast, and all the extremists in the north lining the avenue out to Stormont.'[19]

The protocol of the visit on 14 January 1965 was an awkward point. O'Neill recalled waiting at Stormont three minutes before Lemass' arrival. Should he welcome him to 'Ulster'? Or to 'Northern Ireland'? Both terms might offend the Taoiseach's anti-partition sensibilities. When Lemass's car pulled up, at about 1 pm, O'Neill greeted him with 'Welcome to the North!' and his customary wide smile. Lemass, however, didn't respond, leaving the niceties to his civil service colleague, T. K. Whitaker. Helping Lemass off with his coat, O'Neill asked his guest whether he would like to wash: 'there was a grunt of agreement'. They visited the spacious toilets 'and then, obeying the calls of nature after a long drive, [Lemass] suddenly said, 'I shall get in great trouble for this.' 'No,' I replied, 'it is I who shall get in trouble for this.'"[20] The two men finally relaxed over a pre-prandial drink. It was emphasised to reporters that no political topics were discussed. Lemass, however, did raise the possibility of cross-border joint schemes to attract international business investment.[21] A northern civil servant present, rather naively, concluded that Lemass 'wasn't really interested in politics. He was much more interested in business, and he liked to joke.'[22]

Paisley was quick to react to news of Lemass' arrival and with three colleagues he circled Stormont in a car trailing a huge Union flag.[23] Later, at a meeting in the Ulster Hall, where he launched his 'O'Neill Must Go' campaign, Paisley announced that 'Captain O'Neill has forfeited the right to be our Prime Minister . . . He is a bridge builder he tells us. A traitor and a bridge are very much alike for they both go over to the other side.'[24] From this point on, Paisley harassed O'Neill remorselessly. For the rest of his premier-ship, O'Neill could rarely make a public appearance without enduring the attentions of a shouting crowd of Paisleyite protestors. 'I have been picketed, denounced and traduced as no previous Prime Minister in Northern Ireland's history,' he later admitted.[25]

The summit had a rapid effect on the Nationalist Party. Within a week of the meeting, Eddie McAteer was summoned to Dublin for talks with the Taoiseach. Soon after, the Nationalist Party accepted the position of Official Opposition to the Government at Stormont. Its leaders assuaged their doubts by recalling party policy that in a future united Ireland Stormont would anyway still exist as a federative unit of the nation.[26] Many unionists, however, were concerned about what the meeting might lead to, and suspicious of the secrecy that surrounded it. One Orange Order speaker reminded his audience of the Taoiseach's IRA background: 'Do not forget that Mr Lemass was in the past a gunman and a rebel. He carried a gun against Britain and our own kith and kin.'[27]

Terence O'Neill made the return visit, this time with wives present, to meet Lemass in Dublin in July 1965.[28] This meeting went off without a hitch. Years later, in 1973, Seán Lemass's widow, Kathleen Lemass, made a remarkable claim:

Sean explained to me that they [O'Neill and Lemass] wanted to convey the impression to the outside world that the talks were just about routine matters. In fact, both men wanted to see Ireland united. Their idea was to have several meetings at various levels between Government officials so that co-operation would begin; eventually leading to Irish unity.

Sean normally disliked talking politics at home. But this one time he was really excited and in fact was brimming over with happiness. He told me he had great hopes that things would work out and that he and Captain O'Neill had found a lot of common ground and could talk to each other freely and sensibly without history spoiling things. Captain O'Neill seemed just as happy. On the day of his visit to Dublin

he told me that his intention was to get Ireland united. . ... Very few
people have known until this day that both of those men wanted the
unification of Ireland and I am convinced they could have achieved it.

Naturally O'Neill vehemently denied these claims, and pointed
out inaccuracies in Mrs Lemass's account.[29]

There's no doubt, however, that in some governmental circles
in Britain by the mid-1960s a weakening of partition would have
been a welcome result. In a memorandum to Prime Minister
Harold Wilson, the Commonwealth Secretary wrote:

Our general relations with the Irish Republic have improved consider-
ably in recent years; in the same way, friendly contacts have developed
between Lemass and Captain O'Neill. Looking to the future it would
probably be desirable that partition should be brought to an end and
we even look forward to the day when a reunified Ireland would join
the Commonwealth.[30]

Ambivalence on the border could even be found amongst Ulster
protestants at large. A 1967 survey found 58 per cent of Unionist
voters in favour of the status quo as best for Ireland, but 38 per cent
thought a united Ireland linked to Britain would be better. Leaving
aside preferences, 41 per cent of unionists believed that the border
would eventually disappear.[31] What might O'Neill have thought?
In 1972, O'Neill said that he felt sure that one day there would be a
united Ireland, if not by then in his lifetime.[32]

By 1966, however, O'Neill had cause to regret the early press
optimism.

The sole purpose of my meeting with Mr Lemass was to establish
friendly relations. Mr Lemass said a significant thing when he returned
to Dublin when he said the meeting should not be exaggerated. Idiotic

leaders and articles in the *New York Times* about the 'crumbling wall' had been the cause of much trouble and misunderstanding in regard to the Lemass meeting. If all of you had believed what we both said at the time, there would not have been this trouble.[33]

THE CRISIS OF 1966

It was not surprising that O'Neill had turned pessimistic by 1966. This year was the fiftieth anniversary of the Dublin Easter Rising against British rule. Tensions were high in Northern Ireland. The normally staid *Belfast Telegraph* announced 'an imminent crisis for the whole country'.[34] Stormont placed the police and auxiliary B-Specials on a 'footing of instant readiness' to deal with any possible IRA outbreaks.[35] In the event, commemorations in Northern Ireland went off peacefully (except for some Paisleyite disruption). Organisers had refused to seek permission for them, so they were technically illegal, but the RUC did not interfere. 'Not one policeman was bruised,' as O'Neill later recalled.[36] But many unionists were deeply disturbed that O'Neill had permitted subversive provocation.

No doubt stirred by the reigning paranoia of IRA plotting, loyalist paramilitarism emerged. Over the weekend of 7/8 May 1966 there were three attacks in Belfast. A seventy-seven year old arthritic protestant woman, Matilda Gould, was badly burned when her house, adjacent to a catholic owned pub off the protestant Shankill Road in Belfast, was petrol-bombed. Two minutes later a catholic house was similarly fire-bombed and the following night two petrol bombs were thrown into the grounds of Saint Mary's Teacher Training College on the Falls Road.[37] On 21 May a message from the First Belfast Battalion of the UVF was telephoned to the *Belfast Telegraph*:

From this day on we declare war against the IRA and its splinter groups. Known IRA men will be executed mercilessly and without hesitation. . . We solemnly warn the authorities not to make any more speeches of appeasement. We are heavily armed protestants dedicated to this cause.'[38]

On 22 June it was announced that John Scullion, who had died eleven days previously, was to be exhumed. He had been mortally injured in an alleged stabbing incident over three weeks before, but anonymous callers to the *Belfast Telegraph* now claimed that he had actually been shot by loyalist extremists.[39] In the early morning of 26 June Peter Ward, an eighteen year old catholic bar man, was shot and killed as he left work in a pub on Malvern Street, off the Shankill Road. Two friends were wounded. The RUC subsequently picked up five suspects. The next day Matilda Gould finally died from the wounds received seven weeks earlier.[40]

Suddenly it was clear that a new extremist organisation was at work. Terence O'Neill, who rushed back from the Somme commemoration in France, reacted with unprecedented decisiveness, announcing to Stormont that he was banning the UVF under the Special Powers Act. The following day O'Neill went further and (erroneously) linked Paisley to the new organisation.[41] Police intelligence had convinced O'Neill that an orchestrated campaign of loyalist subversion, stretching from the extremes of his own party all the way to paramilitary murder, was directed against his government.[42]

Early in June 1966, Paisley had marched on the Presbyterian General Assembly in Belfast to protest its 'Romanising' tendencies.[43] As Paisley led nearly 1,000 passed through Cromac Square on the way to the General Assembly, they were attacked by youths from the catholic Markets area. One man, armed with an iron bar, came within a few feet of Paisley. The Paisleyites carried on to the

General Assembly where the Governor, Lord Erskine, and his wife were barracked and jostled.[44] In a twenty minute speech to Stormont, Terence O'Neill likened Paisleyites to the Nazis:

> To those who remember the thirties, the pattern is horribly familiar. The contempt for established authority, the crude unthinking intolerance, the emphasis upon monster processions and rallies, the appeal to a perverted form of patriotism. Each and every one of these things has its parallel in the rise of the Nazis to power. A minority movement was able in the end to work its will, simply because most people were too apathetic or too intimidated to speak out. History must not be allowed to repeat itself in this small corner of the British Commonwealth.

'My family,' O'Neill reminded his listeners, 'has been practically wiped out fighting for the flag' against Nazism, and he warned that 'if a fascist movement were allowed to rule the roost in Ulster, then our constitution might indeed be in danger.'[45] From the Unionist bank-benches, Roy Bradford called Paisley a 'latter-day Luther of the lumen-proletariat, this very small time Savonarola of the Shankill Road.'[46]

Governor Erskine had been particularly targeted by the Paisleyites because of his role in yet another controversy. The Unionist-controlled Belfast Corporation had wished to name a new bridge in Belfast after Carson, hero of Ulster resistance to Home Rule in 1912. The Governor intervened to make clear that the Queen, who was due to open the bridge, didn't wish to get embroiled in the inevitable controversy that would ensue.[47] The Corporation Unionists, much irritated, plumped for the name 'Queen Elizabeth II'.[48] Paisley, meanwhile, had persuaded Carson's son, Edward, to join his campaign protesting the insult to the Unionist hero's name.[49] Carson had written to O'Neill over the bridge controversy but, he said, O'Neill had 'made it clear he didn't like me and didn't want to meet me.'[50] Paisley hoped to stand Carson against the Ulster Unionist Party in the forthcoming Westminster general election, but the challenge fizzled.

The Queen duly visited Belfast to open the bridge on 4 July. As her car passed a tall building under construction on Great Victoria Street, a catholic labourer dropped a concrete block onto the bonnet, denting it to a depth of several inches.[51] O'Neill wrote privately at the time how this incident threw a spanner into his plans to have the Queen publicly approve his bridge-building policy in her farewell speech:

> 'I see', she said, 'that he [Paisley] had ten thousand people listening to him last night.' . . . 'The catholics in Northern Ireland do not like me,' she mused, 'what happens if the protestants also turn against me?' 'Well,' I replied, turning to the Duke, 'the Prime Minister is having a difficult time at the moment with his left wing [the pro-civil rights Campaign for Democracy in Ulster]. What is at stake is, quite literally, the constitutional position of Northern Ireland.' This seemed to impress the Duke – but not her unfortunately. . . . The brick, which by this time the Queen knew had been thrown by a catholic, was enough to ensure that the farewell message was also muffed. The Queen, who in Ulster is more a symbol of protestantism than an ordinary monarch, had failed to use her position in a responsible manner. . . . How can one drag Northern Ireland, kicking and screaming, into the second half of the twentieth century if single-handed, unaided even by one's Queen?[52]

On O'Neill's own initiative the motorcade had travelled through loyalist Sandy Row. Cheering for the monarch was enthusiastic but many booed O'Neill.

On 18 July Paisley was charged with a number of his lieutenants with unlawful assembly, relating to his picket of the Presbyterian General Assembly. One thousand protested outside the court.[53]

Once in Crumlin Road Gaol the martyrs attracted vigils of thousands for two nights running. On the third night it developed into a riot causing extensive damage to property, twenty hospitalisations and sixteen arrests. A water-cannon for riot-control was used for the first time in Northern Ireland.[54] O'Neill's government imposed a three month ban on marches within a fifteen mile radius of the centre of Belfast.[55]

For many Unionists, it was intolerable that their Government should confront loyalists while permitting nationalists to march in celebration of the treasonous 1916 Rebellion. Stormont buildings were now rife with 'secret meetings within the corridors and toilets' plotting against O'Neill.[56] In September, the crisis exploded in the Parliamentary Unionist Party when twelve out of 36 backbenchers signed a petition calling for a new leadership.[57] Faulkner, who had argued for Paisley's right to protest ecumenism outside the Presbyterian General Assembly,[58] was approached by the plotters, met with them three nights in succession, but ultimately refused to wield the knife.[59] The *Unionist* newspaper listed six main areas of concern:

1. O'Neill's meeting with Lemass.
2. The scale of the Easter Rising commemoration parades in Belfast.
3. The imprisonment of Paisley.
4. Persistent resentment in country areas at the scrapping of railways.
5. Land troubles in the New City development area (referring to compensation for mandatory land purchase).
6. The Government's recognition of the Northern Ireland Committee of the Irish Congress of Trade Unions.[60]

At the centre of this rebellion, however, was O'Neill's personal relations with his MPs.

O'Neill was not one to keep his friends closer and his enemies closer. Desmond Boal, the Unionist MP close to Paisley, would later tell his colleagues that he 'had never talked to the Prime Minister nor had the Prime Minister talked to him.' [61] O'Neill was a shy, aloof figure, and even his characteristic whooping laugh unsettled colleagues more than it embraced them. O'Neill was, by accounts, amiable with friends, and had a nice line in self-deprecating humour, but his 'magnificent wit,' as a T. E. Utley recalled, depended 'largely though not wholly on mimicry.' His poking fun at the Ulster brogue of his party colleagues hardly endeared him. [62] Cotralioe de Burgh Kinahan, a friend, thought that the problem was that O'Neill ceased to listen to the sound advice of his wife, Jean, on social skills:

> Terence was very intelligent in many ways, but he had absolutely no 'common touch' or ability to talk to the man on the street, and with his accession to Prime Minister, he lost what little ability he ever had. Many years later I met a builder at an Official Dinner who told me with great pride that he had been instrumental in having a 'Private Toilet' arranged in the Prime Minister's offices as he thought it was appalling that Terence O'Neill should have to walk through the Members' Room to get to one. [63]

O'Neill was often thought to lack the killer instinct. [64] When it came to this direct challenge to his position, however, O'Neill was determined. He had been on holiday while the petition circulated but rushed back to immediately condemn it as a 'conspiracy':

> I have only this to say – I will fight this out; I believe that my policies represent the best safeguard to our constitutional position and our best hope for prosperity. I believe too that the people of Ulster support them. I do not intend to desert all those who have backed me. I fought for my country in time of war. I have fought to maintain our constitution in time of peace. There will be no surrender. [65]

It was clear that he would not go quietly and that he was prepared to appeal to the public against opposition in the party. O'Neill strategy was to link the attack on him with the Paisleyite 'O'Neill Must Go' campaign.[66] As Faulkner recalled, O'Neill represented his critics as 'shell-backed reactionaries'.[67]

On 27 September the decisive Parliamentary Unionist Party meeting was held. Terence O'Neill wore the Red Hand tie-pin of Lord Carson, as donated by the mecurial Edward Carson. Only Desmond Boal openly called on O'Neill to resign, though Faulkner absented himself.[68] One liberal supporter, Peter Montgomery, president of the Arts Council, wrote to O'Neill expressing his delight at the Prime Minister's 'resounding victory over the powers of darkness.'[69]

O'NEILL ISOLATED

O'Neill did move to placate his critics. Senior cabinet disloyalists – Brian Faulkner, William Morgan and Harry West – were left in post, but Brian McConnell was demoted from Minister of Home Affairs to Minister of State in Development and Bill Craig was moved out of the Development into Home Affairs.[70] Craig was much embittered. James Chichester-Clark, a fellow minister, found him drunk in his room, where Craig slurred, 'Well, if Faulkner can be a rebel I'll get to the right of Faulkner, so.'[71] Craig signalled from the outset that he intended to be a 'hard' Minister of Home Affairs: 'It has always been traditional that the Minister of Home Affairs has a special duty to preserve the constitution of Northern Ireland, and that will be my first priority. No one who threatens the constitution from any corner will be overlooked.'[72] He was the wrong man to be Minister of Home Affairs.

Further cabinet upset came later in 1967 when Minister of agriculture Harry West was forced to resign over his handling of a ninety-acre land purchase in County Fermanagh. West felt much aggrieved as he had been simply engaging in customary practices to maintain the sectarian balance. To fellow Unionist MPs he 'talked about the great personal expense to people who lived in the counties west of the [River] Bann in trying to retain property in protestant hands. . . . He spoke of his own case in the buying of the farm and how he had been let down by the Party.'[73] Faulkner, predictably, backed West so far as he could without actually resigning in solidarity.[74]

In an attempt to buy Faulkner's loyalty, O'Neill secretly promised him that he would retire the premiership in September 1969, handing the baton on to Faulkner.[75] West's dismissal, however, convinced Faulkner that O'Neill could not maintain unity in the party and that he, in turn, would be in due course witch-hunted.[76] It also finally shattered O'Neill's relations with his predecessor, Lord Brookeborough, who like West was a Fermanagh politician. In an angry exchange of letters, Brookeborough rebuked O'Neill. What 'really rankled' in his mind was O'Neill's insistence that his was the first progressive Unionist government: 'your constant references to our supine habits was very galling to a late leader of your own party. . . . I have resented being kicked in the teeth, as you have tried to build up your own image.'[77]

Never much inclined to operate through his party, O'Neill now turned even more to public opinion. 'The trouble with these politicians,' he said of his own MPs, 'is that their only contact [is] with certain members of the old Unionist Party clique in their constituency and they are misled by them into thinking the people of Northern Ireland do not welcome the improvement in community relations and in our relations with the South.'[78] O'Neill's next dramatic move was to address the people above the head of his own party.

CHAPTER 4

O'Neill's PEP Pill

From the beginning of his premiership, O'Neill stressed opportunities for people to work together, but he shied away from explicitly addressing catholics. In February 1965, for example, O'Neill had urged 'a community spirit, since no area can afford to be a mere collection of vested interests, with no sense of common purpose.'[1] The prospect of serious disorder around the fiftieth anniversary of the Easter Rising in 1966 spurred O'Neill into broaching head-on the question of community relations. Over the anniversary weekend Terence O'Neill delivered a considered address on 'The Ulster Community' to a joint protestant and catholic conference at the inter-denominational Corrymeela Centre in Ballycastle. Here he argued that while catholic nationalist identity could not simply be wished away, the state must require loyalty of all citizens. But this need not simply be passive acquiescence for the minority:

If we cannot be united in all things, let us at least be united in working together, in a Christian spirit, to create better opportunities for our children, whether they came from the [catholic] Falls Road or from [protestant] Finaghy. In the enlightenment of education, in the dignity of work, in the security of home and family, these are ends which all of us can pursue. As we advance to meet the promise of the future, let us shed the burden of traditional grievance and ancient

resentments. There is much we can do together. It must and – God
willing it – will be done.

O'Neill's ambition, he said, was to encourage everyone to participate in achievements in which all could feel proud. Nationalists,
however, must accept that Northern Ireland would remain unionist,
protestant, and British, and that the Unionist dominance of
Stormont was legitimate.[2]

The response to O'Neill Corrymeela speech was mixed. The
Belfast Telegraph hailed it as the highest point of O'Neill's premiership since he met Lemass.[3] The Nationalist leader, Eddie McAteer,
was understandably less impressed:

> It has all been said before, only much more sincerely. Unquestioning
> catholic allegiance to an Orange government seems to be Captain
> O'Neill's brilliant idea of statesmanship. These long range salvoes of
> goodwill are less effective than one hour of head-to-head discussion on
> practical measures.[4]

O'Neill was not, however, interested in bi-laterals with the
Nationalist Party, which he saw as outmoded and in decline.

As political and civil unrest intensified in Northern Ireland
during 1966, the British Government began to cast a wary and, from
the Unionist point of view, unwelcome eye on the situation.[5] O'Neill
had been aware for some time of the risk of British intervention. As
unionist opposition to modernisation grew, his earlier emphasis on
selling Northern Ireland as a suitable area for investment developed
into a crusade to preserve the province's political image. He warned
the 1965 Unionist conference that if 'we do not take into account the
need to stand well in the eyes of British opinion we will be sticking
our heads in the sand.'[6] This theme was constantly repeated
throughout his struggle with Paisleyism through the year.

PRESSURE FOR REFORM

The Campaign for Social Justice (CSJ), which for three years had been attempting to follow Unionist advice and bring a discrimination case through the courts, in November 1966 was refused necessary legal aid.[7] Blocked in one direction the various organisations began to turn with renewed vigour to developing propaganda for the British market. The nationalist politician, Gerry Fitt, elected to Westminster for West Belfast in April 1966, used his position to flail Stormont for discrimination.[8] Fitt's predilection for hair-raising rhetoric – he warned that unless reform was forthcoming the day could 'arise when Irishmen would find it necessary to shoot brother-Irishmen'[9] – helped O'Neill position himself as a reasonable voice. Still, pressure from London was building. O'Neill met with British Labour Prime Minister Harold Wilson at 10 Downing Street on 3 August 1966. Informal discussion over lunch centred on the Paisleyite movement and its 'violent tendencies', though O'Neill tried to bring attention to the violent intentions of republicans also. In the meeting proper, Wilson insisted that reform must be forthcoming; otherwise 'Westminster would be forced to act.' O'Neill replied that the steps he had taken to 'bring about an atmosphere of reconciliation between opposing sections of the . . . community' were 'a necessary pre-requisite to any concrete action' on reforms. The 1916 commemorations, he said, had produced a 'severe back-lash' amongst elements of the protestant community 'which made it politically impossible to make further moves at present'. Wilson concluded with recognition of 'the changed atmosphere which Captain O'Neill had created since he assumed office and he thought it right in these circumstances to allow him to pursue his new policies without interference from London'.[10]

Asked by journalists about how the summit had gone, O'Neill remarked dryly that electoral reform 'is a difficult thing to discuss with Englishmen.'[11] To his cabinet Terence O'Neill argued that he had won tacit acceptance for a 'pause' in reform, but he emphasised that this had merely 'bought time'. This atmosphere of sober reflection was shattered by Brian Faulkner. He brashly 'wondered what practical action the United Kingdom Government and Parliament could really take.'[12] But the meeting was a watershed. For the first time the British Government had applied direct pressure on the civil rights front. Both the NILP and the Nationalists were confident that reform was now inevitable.[13]

CIVIC WEEKS

On 23 January 1967, only days after the establishment of the Northern Ireland Civil rights association (NICRA), O'Neill launched what he hoped would become a major facilitator of communal reconciliation and social integration. With the Lord Mayor of Belfast he announced that Ulster Weeks, commercial events held in British cities, were to come to Northern Ireland: Belfast, Limavady, Downpatrick, Antrim, Newry, Coleraine, and Derry were all to have their own 'Civic Weeks'. The civic weeks movement would be co-ordinated by a new organisation called Programme to Enlist the People, or PEP. O'Neill explained that 'the whole point of PEP was to encourage the people of each city or town in a spontaneous expression of civic pride, and in developing a new sense of involvement in what the province as a whole was doing.'[14]

This was a return to O'Neill's theme of 'self-help', but mediated through his experience of pushing modernisation. Ructions over the New City, the Second University and trade union recognition had convinced him that, even in small Northern Ireland, there was a gap between people and government that needed to be bridged. Town-based festivals, he hoped, would inculcate a sense of local pride and encourage people to get involved in planning improvements to infrastructure and amenities. Seven towns held Civic Weeks in 1966, twenty-two in 1967, and twenty-two in 1968. They were largely middle class enterprises, organised primarily by Junior Chambers of Commerce.[15] They partook of the decidedly royalist culture of Unionist Northern Ireland. Princess Margaret and her husband, Lord Snowdon, for example, were the guests of honour at Belfast Civic Week.[16] In one civic week, in unconscious anticipation, an army detachment put on a display in which they suppressed a mock riot!

In a major speech in February 1968, O'Neill endeavoured to explain the PEP approach to Northern Ireland's community relations problems. He spoke hopefully of the emergence of 'a broad area of middle ground which can be occupied by reasonable men.' He defended the lack of concrete reform so far: 'people ought to accept that these matters are not just plain sailing . . . Action by words is an essential forerunner in difficult and contentious matters to action in deeds. . . . Tolerance and mutual respect cannot be the subject of legislation: they must stem from the minds and the consciences of individual men and women.'[17] O'Neill's phrase – 'action in words' was telling. It justly acknowledged that improved community relations required the building up of a common culture of communication, and his ambition to thicken the texture of civil society was a plausible way in which to pursue this. But words were a poor alternative to concrete reform when discrimination, gerrymandering and voting restrictions buttressed Unionist domination and penalised catholics.

PEP was a kind of 'big society'. It did not envisage Unionists giving up their near monopoly on the symbolic accoutrements of the state. Nor did it require tangible concessions to meet the civil rights grievances of the minority. Catholics were being asked to participate in an unreformed polity to which they were traditionally hostile and alien. PEP was a positive and broadminded initiative, but it ducked the challenge of a British Unionist state governing citizens who wished to have their Irishness asserted and approved in their own country.

O'Neill hoped that PEP and Civic Weeks would succeed in involving catholics in the 1971 Jubilee celebrations marking fifty years since partition.[18] But his call for civic activism and community activism could be turned against the Unionist government. On 20 June 1968, the young and radical Nationalist Party MP, Austin Currie, squatted in a house in Caledon, protesting at its misallocation to a protestant family. Charles Brett of the NILP saw the irony: 'Captain O'Neill seeks participation by people in public life. In Caledon he has got it – and no wonder.'[19] On 27 September O'Neill made a speech to the PEP committee meeting only days before the eruption of the civil rights 'October '68 revolution'. Ironically, he pointed to youth led radicalism internationally as a sign that the state internationally had become too distant from the people. His PEP pill, he felt sure, could cure the world's malaise.[20] But when the New Left came to Northern Ireland, it was to decisively reject O'Neill's model of civic engagement. A student placard on the Queen's students' sit-down in Linen Hall Street on 9 October read: 'Civil rights, not civic weeks'.[21] Not only radicals were disabused. The Roman Catholic Cardinal Conway rejected Civic weeks as inadequate in March 1969:

> I think many Unionists underestimate the capacity of people to see when they are being fobbed off with words and gestures. Our people are not at all impressed, for example, when civic weeks and visits to Catholic schools seemed to chalked up as much needed reform.[22]

In April 1969 it was reported that the number of towns planning to hold civic weeks in 1969 had slumped 25 per cent on the previous year.[23] As protest, disorder and catholic alienation mounted they quickly foundered.

Feargal Cochrane has argued that O'Neill pursued merely 'feel-good' policies and ducked the sectarianism woven into the state.[24] O'Neill did not entirely limit himself to the 'action in words' of PEP and Civic weeks, however. In the year or so before the civil rights movement broke he made some discreet moves to advance concrete reform. The 1966 Queen's speech, and more so O'Neill's conciliatory gloss which followed, did include real olive-branches. Certain legal reforms were to be undertaken to facilitate the extension of state aid to the catholic-run Mater Hospital. The business vote and the Queen's University seats in Stormont elections were to be abolished, and a boundary commission in time was to re-examine all Stormont constituencies.[25] A review major re-drawing of Belfast constituencies, to general surprise, resulted in no pro-Unionist gerrymander.[26] Funding was increased to voluntary Catholic schools, so that grants covered eighty per cent of costs.[27] It seems that there was even a secret meeting at Unionist headquarters, attended by unionist organisers from across the province, to grapple with the 'Londonderry problem'. Here O'Neill tried to explain the 'new image'.[28] However, Londonderry's Unionists refused to accept any move to reform.[29]

The justice of the charge of timidity and 'too little too late' is undeniable, but it should not detract from O'Neill's initiation of real change, nor the considerable effort and conviction O'Neill had put into his Civic weeks and PEP scheme. O'Neill's view that reconciliation must be actively fostered from bottom-up, and could not be legislated for, was not just a cop-out. PEP was a strikingly coherent and theorised campaign to mobilise civil society to under-mine traditional communal and state-citizen divisions. It was the audacious heart of 'O'Neillism'.

CHAPTER 5

The North Explodes

Well into 1968, it was the Paisleyites above all who threatened disorder. In May 1968 O'Neill addressed Woodvale Unionist Association. As he left the meeting in this intensely loyalist working class area of Belfast he was jeered by a crowd of 500. Stones, bags of flour and eggs were thrown.[1] O'Neill was slightly injured, though as it was an eye wound it could have been serious. But catholic discontent had been steadily welling up. On 24 June 1968, Austin Currie took up the issue of a council house allocation in the town of Caledon, granted to a nineteen year old female protestant, Miss Beatty, in preference to a large catholic family left on the waiting list for years. One thousand attended an open air meeting in Dungannon at which Currie insisted that 'Caledon will not be an end but it will be a beginning unless our demands are satisfied.'[2] When Currie returned to Stormont to open a debate on the matter, all Unionist back benchers filed out.[3] Such a response can only have reinforced for many catholics the seeming pointlessness of pursuing their case through parliament.

THE CIVIL RIGHTS MOVEMENT

On 27 August leftist activists in Derry – principally Eamonn McCann – announced that they had invited the civil rights organisation NICRA to organise a march there.[4] They protested general social deprivation, but also the gerrymandering of Derry's constituencies and the ratepayer' franchise in the local government elections that denied 'one man one vote', in the parlance of the time. Bill Craig as Minister of Home Affairs insisted that the march be re-routed so that it remained pegged back in the catholic district. The town centre was declared off-limits. When the marchers attempted to break the blockade the RUC – many without identity numbers - responded with batons. Two MPs, Eddie McAteer and Gerry Fitt, were amongst the first to be injured. Soon, police water-cannons were spraying indiscriminately in Duke Street and on Craigavon Bridge. A report by three British observers noted that a woman of about sixty 'who was hysterical on the pavement after having been hosed down by water-cannon' had her spectacles removed by a police man with one hand while 'he hit her over the head with his baton with the other.'[5] Rioting spread to the city centre Diamond, then to the catholic Bogside area just outside city walls. As the violence was broadcast on television channels, the civil rights movement erupted. After years of gradual but accelerating tension the dam had burst.

On Sunday 6 October, a group of students picketed the home of William Craig. He irritably dismissed them as 'silly bloody fools'. A subsequent meeting at the Queen University of Belfast established the People's Democracy civil rights group, and announced a march from the university to Belfast city centre for the following Wednesday. The RUC this time thought better of trying to block it, but 1000 Paisleyites forced a re-route by occupying Shaftesbury Square, near the strongly loyalist Sandy Row. When the students arrived at city centre by a circuitous route they founds Paisleyites ensconced in the City Hall area, and in protest staged a sit-down protest at Linenhall Street nearby. Paris had come to Ulster.

O NEILL PUSHES FOR REFORM

O'Neill was immediately consciousness that a full-scale crisis was at hand. He pressed his cabinet to accept 'inescapable facts':

> I would be failing in my duty if I did not make it clear to you that, in my view, Londonderry has dramatically altered the situation to our great disadvantage. Whether the Press and TV coverage was fair is immaterial. We have now become the focus of world opinion . . . Now I ask my colleagues to be realistic about the situation.[6]

O'Neill was launching a campaign to force understanding on his cabinet:

> I think we must be seen to temper firmness with fairness. Of course there are anti-partition agitators prominently at work, but can any of us truthfully say in the confines of this room that the minority have no grievance calling for a remedy?[7]

To convince his colleagues, O'Neill argued for reform as consolidation. O'Neill had long placed great importance on the 1949 Ireland Act promising that partition could not be ended without the assent of the Northern Ireland Parliament. He used this to argue that defence of Stormont was key, and 'things like multiple votes at local government elections . . . are not essential to maintain our position. And we may even in time have to make a bitter choice between losing Londonderry and losing Ulster.'[8] Faulkner and Craig, however presented themselves as the cabinet's strong-men, opposed to concession under 'duress'.[9]

As O'Neill cajoled and the cabinet procrastinated, the civil rights movement spread. A newly formed Derry Citizens Action Committee (DCAC) organised a sit-down protest in the city on 19

October. On the Saturday of 26 October, a small civil rights march from Strabane to Derry was attacked by stick-armed Paisleyites in the protestant town of Magheramason. Three days later there were scuffles in the Derry city council meeting as civil rights protestors took over the chamber. On the first Saturday of November, fifteen members of DCAC symbolically walked the route blocked on 5 October. A Paisleyite Loyal Citizens of Ulster counter-demonstration was led by Major Ronald Bunting sporting an army tunic. (Bunting was right-wing on the constitution, rather left-wing on social issues. Noting high unemployment, low wages and poor housing, he pointed out that it 'is not only the Roman Catholics who are suffering from these things. It is the workers, irrespective of whether they are protestant, catholic, atheist or communist.')[10]

O'Neill, Faulkner and Craig were summoned to meet with Harold Wilson in London on 4 November 1968. Here Wilson threatened 'the complete liquidation of all financial arrangements with Northern Ireland' if reform was not forthcoming.[11] On returning, O'Neill warned his cabinet that while the 1949 Ireland Act guaranteed Northern Ireland's territorial integrity, it did not guarantee subsidies from Westminster. Direct Westminster intervention and the suspension of Stormont was the real threat because 'the maintenance of the overall constitutional position depended upon control at Stormont and not upon the control of certain local authorities in ways which often seem difficult to justify.'[12] He and his allies emphasised the same argument to the Parliamentary Unionist Party. Great Britain provided Northern Ireland with 'a territorial guarantee, but . . . no guarantee on financial assistance'. Ulster's British subsidies – £1 million a year for Harland and Wolff Shipyard, more than £7.5 million for the road building programme, about '£10 million straight . . . on a year to year basis' – could easily be whisked away.[13]

Nonetheless, Craig still preferred repression. O'Neill was furious when, in response to further planned civil rights demonstrations, Craig ordered a month-long ban on all marches within Derry's city walls on 13 November.[14] 15,000 civil rights marchers defied Craig's ban on 16 November. Two days later, 400 dockers and female textile workers struck and marched to show solidarity outside Derry court house with those summonsed for offences arising from 5 October. Meanwhile, with the temporary absence of Faulkner from cabinet meetings (he was on a ministerial visit to Germany) O'Neill took the opportunity to propose a five-point plan to his cabinet.[15] On 20 November, O'Neill ratcheted up the pressure. The cabinet, he argued, should grasp the franchise nettle:

> They had just heard from the police that unless the situation could be cooled down law and order could not be guaranteed; that the franchise issue was the central theme to the Civil Rights movement; that Mr Wilson was now making it clear that if they refused to accept universal adult suffrage, it would be imposed by Westminster legislation. Knowing this, could they in conscience ask the police to face up to a change which Westminster could impose in any case?[16]

When Faulkner returned, however, he was able to rally the cabinet against conceding 'one man one vote' under 'duress'. On 21 November the cabinet, after a series of fourteen arduous meetings, finally agreed a package, *without* 'one man one vote'.[17] A points system for housing allocations was to be adopted and an Ombudsman to deal with complaints appointed. Derry Corporation would be suspended and replaced by a commission. The local government franchise would be examined after the review process was completed in late 1971. Company votes would be abolished. Finally, there would be discussions with the British Government on withdrawing aspects of the Special Powers Act as soon as it could be done 'without undue hazard.'[18] O'Neill, summing-up, congratulated his colleagues 'on the progress which had been made in the direction of reform' but he 'wondered whether the package . . . would be sufficient, in the absence of a commitment to alter the local government franchise, to satisfy the UK Government or to restrain the Civil Rights marchers.'[19] Later, at a meeting of the parliamentary Unionist party, he openly complained that the cabinet had only accepted the five-point reform package as a means of 'getting away with the question of One Man, One Vote'.[20]

ULSTER AT THE CROSSROADS

Protest, indeed, continued. NICRA planned a demonstration in the small cathedral city of Armagh for Saturday 30 November. One thousand Paisleyites were mobilised to occupy the town, and they swarmed in armed with bill-hooks, scythes and pipes hammered to points. The 5,000 civil rights markers were pegged back at police barricades. The Armagh events polarised the Unionist Party; militant resistance to the civil rights movement seemed at least as threatening to civil order.[21] Emboldened, on 4 December O'Neill openly attacked Craig, in particular his stated willingness to defy Westminster interference.[22] Then, at 6 PM primetime on 9 December, Terence O'Neill broadcast to the province, simultaneously on both television channels.[23]

As a senior Stormont civil servant recalled, O'Neill 'loved being on television . . . but his prepared speeches were dreadful, absolutely dreadful.' His speechwriter was Kenneth Bloomfield, who would brook no interference and insisted upon an ornately 'Churchillian' style ill-suited for the intimacy of broadcasting into families' living-rooms.[24] This famous Crossroads Speech certainly reads better in prose than it came across verbally, particularly in O'Neill's stilted and funereally paced tones. But the significance of what he had to say was immediately apparent. He began starkly:

> Ulster stands at the crossroads. . . . I must say to you this evening that our conduct over the coming days and weeks will decide our future.

He criticised the civil rights marchers as 'a minority of agitators determined to subvert lawful authority' who had 'played a part in setting light to a highly flammable material.' But he conceded that 'the tinder for that fire, in the form of grievances real or imaginary, had been piling up for years.' O'Neill argued that his policy had set in train a moderate but 'continuing programme of change'. He repudiated those who believed that the Westminster government could be defied or long held at bay. The only alternative to Stormont leading reform was humiliating intervention from London.

His main concern, however, was to secure 'a swift end to the growing civil disorder throughout Ulster.' The Province stood 'on the brink of chaos' and it was 'simple-minded to believe that problems such as these can be solved by repression.' He called on the civil rights marchers to give the reforms a chance, and to pull-back before they provoked a backlash: 'You are Ulstermen yourselves. You know we are all of us stubborn people, who will not be pushed too far.' The Paisleyites he attacked for their 'bully-boy tactics' in Armagh. He concluded by implicitly offering his resignation unless the broadcast was met by a groundswell of support:

> What kind of Ulster do you want? A happy and respected province in good standing with the rest of the United Kingdom? Or a place continually torn apart by riots and demonstrations and regarded by the rest of Britain as a political outcast? As always in a democracy, the choice is yours. . . . But if you should want a separate, inward-looking

and divided Ulster then you must seek for others to lead you along that road, for I cannot and will not do it.[25]

O'Neill had wished to give the impression of taking the people into his confidence. His delivery hardly suited the purpose – he intoned rather than conversed – but the response was extraordinary none-theless. The civil rights organisations were much more impressed by the broadcast and the subsequent sacking of Craig than they had been by the 5 point reform programme. They announced a month-long 'truce' during which marches and demonstrations would cease. It also impressed the audience south of the border. On 29 December, the southern Irish *Sunday Independent* named Terence O'Neill as their 'Man of the Year'. In total about 125,000 wrote to support O'Neill, 77,836 on *Belfast Telegraph* coupons and 47,000 directly to Stormont.[26] The equivalent in Britain would have been almost seven million letters.[27] O'Neill eyed these potential recruits to Unionism. But his first move was to sack an increasingly troublesome William Craig from the government.

BURNTOLLET

O'Neill's good cheer was soon broken when a People's Democracy march, which set-off from Belfast to Derry on New Year's Day 1969, in defiance of the civil rights 'truce', was attacked by loyalists (including out-of-uniform members of the police reserve B-Specials) at Burntollet Bridge. Rioting followed in Derry, and after the RUC rampaged through the nationalist Bogside they had to be withdrawn from the area for a week. Clearly loyalists and the police were the aggressors here. The loyalist threat was palpable. In south Derry County, where the Paisleyite Ulster Protestant Volunteers claimed 5 – 6,000 supporters, one moderate Unionist businessman reported that 'up until the [Burntollet] march you could joke with friends about Paisley, but you keep quiet now. No one feels free to talk, because it's safer that way.'[28] Unionists, however, were far more concerned that catholics in Derry were battling police. Particularly galling was a mural that went up at the Leckey Road in the Bogside proclaiming 'You are now entering Free Derry'. The seditious and ill-disciplined minority seemed to be reverting to type. The Derry Unionist MP Albert Anderson would later quiet a rowdy Unionist meeting with the admonishment: 'Don't let us get down to the Leckey Road level . . . let us be the decent protestant people we are.'[29]

O'Neill was clearly caught up in the mood of unionist anger, and his statement on Burntollet had none of the balanced sang-froid of the 'Ulster at the Crossroads' broadcast:

> Enough is enough. We have heard sufficient for now about civil rights, let us hear about civic responsibility. For it is a short step from the throwing of paving stones to the laying of tombstones and I for one can think of no cause in Ulster today which will be advanced by the death of a single Ulster-man. . . . The march to Londonderry planned by the so-called People's Democracy was from the outset a foolhardy and irresponsible undertaking. . . . Some of the marchers and those who supported them in Londonderry itself have shown themselves to be mere hooligans ready to attack the police and others.

Unless protestors left the streets, O'Neill warned, the B Specials would be mobilised.[30] Roy Bradford, a close ally of O'Neill in the cabinet, hinted that the student grants of student activists might be cut and the right to protest curtailed: 'Let us not delude ourselves. The ideal state of freedom of protest is not compatible with political realities in Northern Ireland. . . . The present campaign is engineered and activated by political and not social forces. It is designed to overthrow, if not the Union . . . then certainly the Unionist Government.'[31] In face of such vituperation and threats, doubly offensive to civil rights marchers as they had been the victims rather than the aggressors, the 'truce' collapsed.

People's Democracy organised a march in Newry for the following Saturday. The RUC demanded a re-route, as part of a surreptitious deal with the Paisleyites.[32] A ten person deputation from Newry, including three protestant clergymen and two Unionist councillors, urged the Minister of Home affairs to allow the original route as long as there was no opposition.[33] The cabinet discussed the matter: 'Some Ministers asked whether it was wise to risk possible trouble for the sake of a comparatively minor re-routing, bearing in mind that those along the proposed route did not appear to be objecting to the march. It was decided, however, that this was a decision which could only be properly made by the police.' Clearly there was also a tactical political rationale. The Attorney General trusted that arrests on the spot would have a 'salutary effect'.[34] O'Neill was in no mood to exert himself in defence of the PD right to march.

When the demonstration was duly blockaded by the RUC, demonstrators ran riot and attacked the police. For the first time, civil rights marchers had abandoned the restraint of non-violence, albeit in defiance of their leaders' admonitions. 'Police tactics were clearly to let the wreckers discredit the movement,' the journalist Barry White observed, 'and vandals were playing right into their hands.'[35] This was a propaganda coup for the government. Civil rights radicalism was temporarily discredited. In effect, the pre-Burntollet truce was reinstated, only days after it had broken down.[36]

CAMERON COMMISSION

Given a breathing space, O'Neill recovered his reformist courage
and renewed his offensive on the vexed issue of 'one man one vote'.
In a marathon cabinet session on 15 January he proposed a special
commission to look into the origins and course of the disorders, on
the specific understanding that it would duly recommend early
concession of universal suffrage in the local government franchise.
This was a ploy to get around the pledge in the Unionist Party's last
election manifesto that there would be no reform to the franchise
until the scheduled review of local authority structures was completed in 1971. O'Neill (as ever) was opposed by Faulkner, who feared
that a commission would 'too easily develop into a fundamental,
far-reaching and potentially highly embarrassing inquest into
every aspect of Northern Ireland affairs.'[37] Faulkner proposed
instead that an ultimatum be put to the Unionist Party: franchise
reform or the Government's resignation. The Cabinet plumped
for a commission and in due course Lord Cameron, a Scottish
judge, was appointed as chair.

Given that the commission had to be hard-hitting if it was to
have the authority to force through radical reform, it was set-up
with little regard for Unionist sensibilities. One of the three com-
missioners was a veteran critic of the Stormont regime who had
written an excoriating expose, *Orange Terror in Ulster*, in the 1930s.
Unionists were right to fear that they had made a cross for their
own backs. By the time the Cameron Report was published in
September 1969, events had moved on and 'one man one vote' had
long been conceded. Though deprived of its original Machia-
vellian rationale, the Report nonetheless laid-out in merciless
detail Stormont's failings, and was soon legendry as the authoritative indictment of Unionist rule in Northern Ireland. It has remained
a key historical document ever since. O'Neill's manoeuvre, as

Faulkner had feared, succeeded only in writing Stormont's epitaph and condemnation.

At the time it was set up, however, the Parliamentary Unionist Party was generally favourable to the commission, particularly as it was allied with extra law and order measures.[38] Nationalists and civil rights leaders also welcomed the package, John Hume being convinced that the commission would recommend the concession of remaining civil rights demands.[39] The *Belfast Telegraph* with satisfaction observed the 'speed with which the latest Government initiative on civil rights has cooled passions . . . the best indication yet of the deep-rooted desire of most people to see a peaceful solution. We have had a good look over the brink and it has had a salutary effect.'[40]

Faulkner had been brooding, however. On 24 January he resigned from the cabinet over the establishment of the inquiry commission which he described as a 'political manoeuvre and to some extent an abdication of authority'. He preferred the immediate concession of universal suffrage on the government's own authority. O'Neill's public reply to Faulkner's resignation was astonishingly bitter.[41] O'Neill implied that the minister was merely attempting to embarrass his chief, and he bitterly reflected on the years of disloyalty he had endured at Faulkner's hands:

> You also tell me that you have 'remained through' what you termed 'successive crises'. I am bound to say that if, instead of passively 'remaining' you had on occasions given me that loyalty and support which a Prime Minister has a right to expect from his deputy, some of the so-called 'crises' might never have arisen.

Faulkner felt obliged to reply to this broadside, but did not deign to comment on his support or otherwise for O'Neill in office to avoid 'recrimination'. O'Neill wrote another slashing reply. Had Faulkner shown loyalty 'it would both have sustained me and I am sure increased respect for you.' Faulkner's letters were brief and dignified; O'Neill's lengthy and boiling with ill-concealed rage. Yet, reviewing the period under discussion, it is hard not to sympathise with the beleaguered Prime Minister against his artful second in command.

THE CROSSROADS ELECTION

Faulkner's resignation from the cabinet, followed by that of right-wing minister William Morgan, brought the Unionist Party crisis to a head. On the night of 30 January a petition was handed to party secretary, signed by twelve back benchers, calling for O'Neill's resignation. Most signatories convened at Portadown under Craig's leadership – the 'Portadown Parliament' – on 1 February, where they issued a list of demands. They opposed the commission plan, called for O'Neill's replacement, and insisted that no general election should be called: 'The matter can only be resolved within the party. A general election now would be an act of irresponsibility and would widen the divisions among Unionists.'[42] Sniffing fear amongst his opponents, O'Neill two days later called a general election for 24 February 1969.[43]

In his crossroads broadcast O'Neill had ruled out a general election as likely to inflame passions during a sensitive time. But he had decided now on a make-or-break initiative calculated to split his party and marginalise the traditionalists he saw as irredeemably sectarian: 'I say that a spurious unity secured by a sacrifice of principle is a snare and a delusion. I do not want people merely to support this great party of ours. I want them to respect it.'[44] As the campaign progressed, O'Neill inched ever closer to an explicit appeal for catholic support. 'The best way to protect the constitution,' he insisted, 'not just for our time but for generations to come, is to rally support from every section of Ulster.' The unity of

Ulster, therefore, must come before the unity of the Unionist Party.[45] On the eve of calling the election O'Neill told a rally in Newtownards that 51 per cent of school students were catholic: 'If you are going to go on encouraging them to vote Nationalist, then Ulster will be lost. So we must have a Unionist Party which the people in the country can support.'[46]

O'Neill was struggling to campaign against half of Unionism, a difficult position for its official leader. Tony Geraghty of the *Sunday Times* reported that

> The Prime Minister of Northern Ireland is . . . infiltrating his own party. He is doing this through groups of 'unofficial' Unionists now springing up all over the province in constituencies held by his enemies. These guerrilla bands are well briefed, curiously alike in their tactics and organisation, and all inspired by the desire to preserve Mr Terence O'Neill for the nation.[47]

The response to his Crossroads broadcast allowed O'Neill such autonomy from the formal structures of the Ulster Unionist Party.

The same day O'Neill called the election, a large advertisement appeared in the press, headed 'I back O'Neill,' listing groups complete with chairmen and secretaries in forty-three out of the fifty-two constituencies across the province. It had been paid for by 'Ulster businessmen'.[48] A few days after the election was announced, about 100 well known personalities of various religious denominations and political parties launched a movement to support O'Neill and his objectives: the New Ulster Movement (NUM). Led by Brian Walker, a former spokesperson of the Churches Industrial Council, and Brian McGuigan, a prominent catholic conciliator, the NUM called on the non-party to involve themselves in politics and pledged to support pro-O'Neill candidates. Moderates, it urged, should abandon present allegiances, to the Liberal Party or the NILP for example, because 'the stark choice facing every citizen in Northern Ireland is whether we have a reasonable moderate Unionist Government led by Captain Terence O'Neill and his declared supporters, or a highly unreasonable and reactionary Government led by extremists.'[49] A liberal author, Mary McNeil, was transfixed:

> This ferment from below is really quite astonishing – first it was the Civil Rights people – now it is the New Ulster Movement . . . working day and night . . . organising support for any and every pro O'Neill candidate . . . money *pouring* in – catholics and protestants working together politically for the first time in their lives.[50]

As middle and upper-class arrivistes – described as 'High Tories' by the NILP[51] – flooded into Unionist associations, anti-O'Neill MPs were put on the back foot, and a good many repudiated earlier anti-O'Neill statements. Only three, however, were actually deselected (including William Morgan).

After the nominations closed the NUM announced it was backing pro-O'Neill independents against official Unionist candidates in ten constituencies.[52] Most supporters and election workers for these candidates were not Unionist Party members.[53] Pro-O'Neill Ulster Unionists, meanwhile, argued for a splitting of the party. Robin Bailie was the Unionist candidate for the Newtownabbey constituency in Belfast. Observing the discomfiture of the anti-O'Neill faction during the election campaign, he urged their formal exclusion from the Unionist movement:

> To imagine that these people can be contained in a single party is nonsense . . . One hopes that this will be a reality that will be recognised by constituency associations and the Unionist Council. . . . The necessary changes which some constituency parties failed to

make to bring the party into tune with the realities of the present day are now being brought about by public opinion in the country.[54]

No pro-O'Neill unionist candidates, either independent or Ulster Unionist, were catholic. Louis Boyle, a youthful catholic who had been a Unionist Party member for some years, and brother of a PD leader, was manoeuvred by the party out of standing in South Down.[55] It was said, however, that Boyle had received 'valuable encouragement and support' from O'Neill.[56]

At the Unionist Party's official manifesto launch, attended by some sixty journalists from Britain, Europe and America, O'Neill avoided dissociating himself from pro-O'Neill independents and promised that the manifesto 'will be available to all who want to use it.' He refused to endorse official Unionist candidates opposed to him.[57] The Manifesto itself was full of warm, embracing language, but it shied away from any direct appeal to catholics. Once again, Faulkner out-flanked O'Neill by explicitly calling for catholics to support him personally in his constituency manifesto. Mary McNeil wrote:

> O'Neill came out with a very good manifesto on Friday sticking very well to his points of principle. Then the whole thing is blurred again by Faulkner issuing a manifesto of his own on Saturday in which he out-does O'Neill in his stand for principles – whereas O'Neill said he wanted cooperation from everyone in N. Ireland – not specifically mentioning Roman Catholics – Faulkner calls for them by name and says how many friends he has among them in East Down!! It is wicked of him, for if he had supported O'Neill in December there would have been none of these cabinet crises.[58]

Faulkner had played another masterful stroke to flank O'Neill, but the truth was that most Unionists simply did not believe that a new pro-union political party, embracing catholics and splitting from protestant hardliners, could ever be as solid as the old pan-protestant alliance. As one anti-O'Neill Unionist put it, 'Captain O'Neill talks about uniting all Ulster, which is a marvellous thing. Nobody wants this more than I do, but it is just not possible.'[59]

THE BANNSIDE CONTEST

O'Neill was distracted by the necessity of defending his own seat. For the first time in his career, he faced a contest in his constituency of Bannside. At a 2,000 strong rally in the Ulster Hall on 1 February Paisley announced his intention to contest O'Neill's seat at the forthcoming general election.[60] Roy Bradford, effectively O'Neill's spokesman during the campaign, predicted that in the public eye the general election would become reduced 'to the symbolic battle of Bannside.'[61] This was hardly such a cause for satisfaction. Paisley proved to be a most effective campaigner. On 19 February a crowd of 2,000 waited in freezing weather to hear him speak in small Ahoghill, O'Neill's home town.[62] In contrast Bannside Unionist association was underdeveloped. The Kells and Connor branch, for example, had ceased to exist sixteen years previously.[63] Facing little opposition in his own constituency of Mid-Antrim, Robert Simpson MP had to be drafted in to chair the 'I back O'Neill' committee in the Prime Minister's constituency and to lead his re-election campaign.[64]

Terence O'Neill's poor campaigning skills were a major hindrance. Asked why he hadn't talked about the issues with workers whilst touring the Frazer and Houghton bleach works in Cullybackey, he responded, 'I don't like to talk politics. I like them to vote for my politics'.[65] A reporter compared his technique with that of Bill Craig's:

Terence O'Neill, cast by the world at large as the boy hero of Ulster, shifts uneasily, looks over his left shoulder, and tortures out a sentence or two. Bill Craig, billed as the starring heavy, suddenly illuminates and goes into the act essential to any serving politician. . . .

Mr O'Neill, facing the ordeal for the first time in his previously uncontested political career, seems to favour the factory visit, though he gets round to the door knocker as well. There is a curious air of embarrassment about the whole business, which spreads around him like some Old Testament plague. He is really much more at home with a policy than a person, as is evident from every encounter.

'My goodness.' He proclaims to the typing pool, 'it's nice and warm in here today. This is the right place to be today.' No one can fault it as an opening remark except that it is so generalised in thought and aim as to be almost incapable of response. So all it draws are those sort of smiles which ask where the nearest door is.

In the sheds he is introduced to individual workers – the supervisors a bit too often – but seems unable to concentrate on the particular man or woman. Within seconds he has absorbed himself in the product or the machine. But chattering iron work does not yet have the vote, and the man in charge of it does.

. . . as he stands saying goodbye to the factory manager a couple of hidden voices shout 'Up Paisley!' You know it is of little significance, but somehow you cannot imagine someone shouting 'Up O'Neill!' after Bill Craig.[66]

O'Neill's patrician awkwardness was magnified by his wider mobilised support base. He had many allies desperately anxious to break through to the catholic vote, but their archaism and lack of democratic savvy left them ill-equipped. The Marquis of Hamilton, Westminster MP for Fermanagh and South Tyrone, was at the centre of a family net-work that provided many pro-O'Neill candidates in rural areas. His vitriolic outburst against Craig's 'Portadown

Parliament' was ill-judged: 'The Portadown hate teach-in surpassed even the crudest tactics adopted at times of frustration by the left-wing element of the Labour Party. In fact, the Portadown junta's behaviour was totally alien to western civilisation.'[67] This was not a man comfortable with modern democratic politics. Similarly, Robert Grosvenor, the fabulously wealthy Duke of Westminster who formed a pro-O'Neill committee in rural south Ulster, referred to the 'Portadown Parliament' as 'the twelve little nigger boys.'[68]

O'Neill's Unionist opponents sneered at the well-heeled ingénues filling out Prime Minister's ranks. In Fermanagh, Harry West identified the support for the O'Neillites as coming overwhelmingly from the middle class: 'There is a very, very, very small minority of Unionists in Fermanagh who are pro-O'Neill. These are mainly people found among the imports – people like teachers and the professional classes.' Captain John Brooke, the anti-O'Neill Unionist candidate (and Lord Brookeborough's son) proudly claimed that 'we are the peasant party. I recognise that there is a considerable star-studded banner on the other side. There are a lot of coronets knocking around, some of them cracked.'[69] Albert Anderson, Unionist MP for Londonderry City, attacked his O'Neillite opponent, Peter Campbell for his privileged background and elite support. 'I fight for a united Unionist Party,' he proclaimed, 'not one divided by class or cheque book.'[70] Campbell, married to Lady Moyra, was brother-in-law of the Marquis of Hamilton.[71]

The pro-O'Neill 'Silent Unionists' candidate opposing Faulkner in the East Down seat was Lieutenant-Colonel Denys Rowan-Hamilton, resident of Killyleagh Castle.[72] Faulkner made much play of his opponent's class background: 'I have seen in my own constituency for the first time in twenty years a class war developing. It is a most regrettable and tragic development.'[73] Faulkner scorned the 'influence of the higher orders, private fortunes or . . . what is termed the more intellectual members of the community' in the O'Neill camp.[74] O'Neill responded angrily, pointing out that Faulkner owned a 'country estate' and was a 'master of foxhounds'.[75] But his self-defence was unconvincing: 'I resent tremendously the suggestion that I associate only with people who have handles to their names and am against the ordinary people. I have tremendous support in the poorest streets of Belfast.'[76]

PRO–O'NEILL CATHOLICS?

O'Neill believed that pre-election opinion-polls indicating wide catholic support for pro–O'Neill candidates promised 'a potential triumph of a wider Unionism.'[77] Terence O'Neill's last election broadcast was full of hope for a re-founded unionism and Northern Ireland:

> I am asking you to put our old religious divisions aside to work together for the good of the country. . . . Let us repair our damaged reputation in Britain and the world. Let us show what a divided Ulster could achieve – which has been remarkable – a united Ulster can surpass. . . . I believe passionately that Northern Ireland must remain an integral part of the United Kingdom. But that status can never be secure as long as a large section of our population sets its face against it. I believe there are few of you indeed who do not appreciate the benefits of the British connection.[78]

A big turn-out for O'Neill by catholics seemed a real possibility. O'Neill claimed on canvassing a 'most marvellous reception in the catholic areas of my constituency and also in Belfast as well. If this is an indication of catholic support the pro–O'Neill candidates are going to get massive support.'[79] An eve-of-poll survey found that 28 per cent of catholics thought that they would vote Unionist, more than for the NILP or Nationalist Party. In another poll, 91 per cent of catholics favoured O'Neill as Prime Minister, as against only 58 per cent of protestants. Ominously, however, it was also reported that 'Many catholics resent the way Captain O'Neill was ready to turn the non-party groundswell of support he received after his television broadcast in December into a Unionist recruiting campaign.'[80]

When the results came in, thirty-nine unionist members had been returned, the largest number since 1921. It is certainly true that the liberal vote had consolidated behind O'Neillite unionism. The NILP had been, as it feared, crushed by 'the O'Neill steam-roller'.[81] Twenty-four pro-O'Neill official Unionists were returned with 32 per cent of the vote. Official anti-O'Neill Unionists returned twelve with 16.2 per cent. Pro-O'Neill Independents returned three with 12.9 per cent. Overall the liberal unionists had done very well in building a vote, but nowhere near well enough to transform unionist representation. Two right-wingers came close to defeat at their hands, Joe Burns and Bill Craig, but they survived. Only one of the ten 'Portadown Parliament' dissidents was actually defeated. The three successful independent pro-O'Neill candidates weren't admitted to the Parliamentary Unionist Party.

On the opposition side, no People's Democracy candidates were victorious, though they polled credibly. John Hume, leader of the Derry civil right movement ousted the veteran Nationalist Party leader, Eddie McAteer. Ivan Cooper, a protestant and former Unionist Party activist converted to civil rights, took another Nationalist seat (in contrast, no catholic unionist was nominated, never mind elected). Harry Diamond, Republican Socialist MP for the Falls constituency in Belfast, lost to Paddy Devlin of the NILP. While the NILP was pro-partition, Devlin's appeal rested on his civil rights activism and former internment as an IRA sympathiser. While O'Neill had counted on an electoral revolution re-making Unionism, the actual revolution took place in nationalist politics. Civil rights militancy over nationalist abstention had been vindicated.

The percentage who voted unionism of all shades was, by statistical chance, 67.4 per cent, *exactly* equal to the percentage of protestants in the electorate.[82] The catholic unionist vote was insignificant. In the end, helped by the proliferation of People's Democracy candidates in previously uncontested seats, catholics had voted, but not for O'Neill's unionism. Most crushingly for O'Neill, in Bannside Michael Farrell, the People's Democracy candidate, soaked up the catholic vote, polling 2,310. O'Neill was only able to defeat Paisley, the man who had dogged his steps with abuse and invective for years, by the relatively narrow margin of 1,411.[83]

END GAME

O'Neill had told the *Washington Post* in January 1969 that 'What I have been trying to do is to persuade Catholics in Northern Ireland that they have a place within the United Kingdom. I have been succeeding, first with the professional class, and gradually with the artisans. I don't believe Catholics in Ulster want to be governed by the Republic of Ireland.'[84] Now he felt let-down, and he blamed country constituencies like his own.[85] He felt personally betrayed by the Bannside result. This bitterness was evident also in his attitude to the catholic electorate: 'Although there was catholic support after my television broadcast it does not seem to have translated itself to the polling booths to the same extent. They are prepared to write letters of support but they are not reached the stage of putting an X against your name.'[86] O'Neill's morale was crushed. He wished to re-sign immediately after the election but was dissuaded by ministers.[87]

O'Neill's campaigning against his own party left him dangerously exposed once the Unionist Party MPs reassembled. 'This has been a bitter election,' said John Taylor MP, 'The Party was split from top to bottom.'[88] MP for Londonderry, Albert Anderson, insisted that in supporting Independents in the election O'Neill '[had] broken the rules and regulations of the party and if any member of the party does that sort of thing he should be chucked out.'[89] (He also attacked him for the temerity of canvassing a catholic area in the city.)[90] Terence O'Neill half-heartedly hoped for an influx into party ranks to his advantage:

> Whatever else recent events may or may not have done they have created a new dimension of interest in politics. All over the country thousands of people who never took the slightest interest in politics before want to join Unionist Associations and play their part. As a party, we should not merely accept this trend, but welcome it. We should take this historic opportunity to renew and strengthen the fabric of Unionism.[91]

In fact, the party was being purged of its liberals.[92] Pro-O'Neill stalwarts, such as the Duke of Westminster, the Earl of Erne, and H. Archdale Porter, were expelled from the party for supporting anti-O'Neill candidates in the election.[93] Even then, ten MPs walked out on O'Neill at the first post-election meeting of the Parliamentary Unionist Party.

Northern Ireland was now firmly set on the path to the 'Troubles'. Some scholars, such as Thomas Hennessy and Simon Prince, have fixed responsibility for the descent into violence firmly on naively leftist civil rights agitators who stirred the sectarian hornets' nest.[94] But it is as well to remember Lenin's dictum that crisis erupts when the discontented 'do not want to live in the old way' and the ruling elites 'cannot carry on in the old way.' O'Neill's had attempted to replace a Northern Ireland based upon segregation of catholic and protestant with one that assimilated middle class catholics into a new non-sectarian unionism. But catholics found deeply offensive the implication that their Irishness was backward and ephemeral. They took it as an intolerable affront that in their country of birth first-class citizenship had to be earned as 'British rights for British citizens'. The residents of a catholic street in Belfast responded to O'Neillite claims on their support by insisting on their 'right to be Irish and anti-Unionist'.[95]

As for the crisis of the ruling order, the disruption of the ruling Unionist Party is crucial in understanding the evolution of disorder in Northern Ireland. It is more important, in this regard, than the Burntollet march, which is usually seen as the 'point of no return'. There had been eleven significant civil rights demonstrations between the Derry march of 5 October 1968 and the issuing on 22 November of the 5-point reform plan. Then two more (including the Armagh stand-off) before O'Neill's 'crossroads' broadcast on 9 December. The following 'truce' lasted twenty-one days, until 1 January, when People's Democracy set off on their 'long march' from Belfast to Derry. After violence at the succeeding 11 January Newry march, however, a planned civil rights march in Strabane was called off. There were no more civil rights demonstrations until O'Neill called the 'crossroads election' on 4 February (except for one day when a small number of Oxford university students turned up to show solidarity in Belfast on 25 January). During the election campaign, civil rights activists threw themselves into canvassing. The 'truce', therefore, had effectively resumed after Newry, and continued to hold for almost two months. Demonstrations only resumed with a PD picket of Stormont on 4 March, and this was followed by another ten notable civil rights (or republican) demonstrations by 18 April – the date of a mile-stone by-election in Mid-Ulster. The pattern is clear. It was the crisis of the ruling party, and the perceived victory of the anti-O'Neill right, that kicked off street agitation in March 1969 at a level not seen since October–November the previous year. Contrary to most accounts, the Burntollet ambush, and by extension the radicalism of PD, should not be seen as the turning-point in the unravelling of order. The crossroads election was key. As Gerry Fitt had put it after the election:

> The hard-line element in the Unionist ranks has been strengthened. But those who are the victims of the hard-line attitude are just not prepared to accept it any longer, and if it persists, there must be a direct confrontation – a head-on collision. It will be back to the streets again.[96]

Now, however, the atmosphere of impending violence was much greater than it had been in 1968.

RESIGNATION

Bernadette Devlin, a youthful PD leader supported by republicans, won the Westminster Mid-Ulster seat from the Unionists on 18 April. This triggered a serious escalation. The RUC, exhausted by continual duty and outraged at the radical civil rights triumph, fought with demonstrators in Derry and then once more punitively invaded the catholic Bogside. Loyalists, meanwhile, bombed the Silent Valley water reservoir, which supplied Belfast, and an electricity pylon near Loughgall in County Armagh.[97] Their intention was to have the IRA blamed (the RUC duly obliged) and to force O'Neill's resignation. In its own terms, this was perhaps the single most effective terrorist attack of the Troubles. O'Neill later was to say that the bombs 'quite literally blew me out of office'.[98]

Privately, as he confided to his cousin Phelim O'Neill, the Prime Minister now thought that the devolved government at Stormont was probably doomed.[99] His immediate reaction, however, was to demand immediate concession of 'one man one vote' from his cabinet, using the escalating crisis to concentrate minds. The ministers James Chichester-Clark and William Long had hitherto opposed such a concession, but now they appeared to 'bow to the general will,' as O'Neill observed. The cabinet's decision was promptly made public to prevent second thoughts.[100] O'Neill then threatened to resign immediately if the wider party refused to accept the reform.[101] The parliamentary Unionist party was deeply unhappy with the concession, one MP predicting 'a protestant revolution'.[102] James Callaghan, the British Home Secretary, had to deliver an ultimatum threatening intervention by Westminster.[103] Unionist MPs grudgingly accepted immediate concession of franchise reform by twenty-eight votes to twenty-two. Faulkner, with astute hypocrisy given that he had called for 'one man one vote' to embarrass O'Neill, now criticised the decision as steamrollering 'the party in the country'.[104]

Chichester-Clark, MP for the rural constituency of South Derry, had begun to be spoken of as a leadership contender since January.[105] He had for some time been positioning himself as Terence O'Neill's heir apparent, saying that he would serve neither under Faulkner nor Craig but would assume the premiership himself if 'the entire Parliamentary Party and Prime Minister wanted it.'[106] Now Chichester-Clark resigned from the cabinet over the concession's 'timing'. He had told his parliamentary colleagues that 'if we decided on one man one vote we could have serious trouble from our own people . . . some formula should be found for a way out of the present situation.'[107] Understandably, O'Neill considered Chichester- Clark to be a weak-willed trimmer.[108]

On Monday 28 April 1969 Terence O'Neill heard two more Unionist MPs were about to defect to the dissident camp. So as to have some influence over who succeeded him, he announced his resignation while the 'moderate' majority still tenuously existed.[109] Bonfires were lit on the protestant Shankill Road in Belfast to celebrate. In his resignation broadcast, O'Neill reflected on his legacy:

> . . .any leader who wants to follow a course of change can only go so far. For change is an uncomfortable thing to many people and inevitably one builds up a barrier of resentment and resistance which can make further progress impossible. . . . But I have no regrets for the six years in which I sought to break the chains of ancient hatreds. I have been unable to realise during my period of office all that I had sought to achieve. Whether now it will be achieved in my lifetime I do not know. . . . No solution based on the ascendancy of any section of our community can hope to endure. Either we live in peace, or we have no life worth living.[110]

That evening O'Neill and Jim Malley, his private secretary, visited the Newsboys Club off York Street. O'Neill recorded: 'After presiding at the annual meeting we go upstairs for the entertainment. Just before taking my seat a large ex-naval chap comes up and, failing to speak, with tears in his eyes, he lifts up my right hand to his lips and kisses it – obviously he is a catholic. It is moving and it is a suitable exit.'[111] Here was O'Neill at his most patrician, but it is of significance that symbolically he took his leave from an assumed representative of the down-trodden catholics rather than his 'own people'.

O'Neill did not want Chichester-Clark to succeed him as Prime Minister. This is despite the legend that he parachuted in his 'cousin' (in fact, one had to go back to 1600 to find a common ancestor). O'Neill tried to persuade John Andrews, the low-key

Leader of the Senate and nominal Deputy Prime Minister to run. Andrews declined, however, and only 'in desperation' did O'Neill turn to Chichester-Clark.[112] O'Neill was determined to block Brian Faulkner, the choice of the Unionist rank and file. When it came to the vote, the Parliamentary Unionist Party was split down the middle. O'Neill's vote was key. Chichester-Clark won seventeen votes to Faulkner's sixteen. O'Neil had voted not for Chichester-Clark, but against Faulkner. There's little doubt that O'Neill thought that 'O'Neillism' was over and would not be carried on under any leader. As far as he was concerned, his bourgeois support-base had failed to break the mould of politics. As he put it shortly after his resignation, 'While good men sleep and honest men play their golf and their bridge, these others, with unwavering zeal, are chipping away at the foundations of our democracy.'[113]

CHAPTER 6

Legacy

O'Neill's ouster convinced many on the catholic side that Stormont was now under the sway of hardliners entirely hostile to them. This had direct influence on the radicalisation of the anti-partition republican movement that would eventuate in the fateful emergence of the Provisional IRA by 1970.[1] Republican militarism, and an ideology that took for granted the essentially reactionary character of unionism in all its forms, ignited a brutal conflict with crown forces that drove Northern Ireland close to civil war in the 1970s and contested Britain's military might into the 1990s.

SHAPING A REPUTATION

O'Neill had hoped for a more positive legacy than this. In November 1968, his civil servant advisor, Kenneth Bloomfield, arranged with the London publisher Faber to produce a book of O'Neill's speeches as the 'first fairly definitive statement of the nature of "O'Neillism"'. (As Bloomfield was O'Neill's speech-writer, he was no doubt keen to see his crafted prose immortalised between hardback covers). The title for the volume initially suggested was 'O'Neill of Ulster', with a subtitle either 'Man of Vision' or 'Man of Moderation'. Faber wisely demurred, and in the midst of the crossroads election campaign of February 1969, 'Ulster at the Crossroads' was finally agreed upon. At one point the title 'Ulster Today and Tomorrow' had been considered, but with the failure of the crossroads election and then O'Neill's resignation the tone had turned definitely valedictory. Bloomfield wrote the commentary linking speech extracts, while John Cole, an editor of *The Guardian* in London, himself born in Northern Ireland, provided an admiring if pessimistic introduction.[2] The book came out in 1969, and was re-printed within the year. Topics covered included 'Community Relations', 'Self-Help: Ulster weeks and PEP', and 'Northern Ireland and the United States'.

Self-sabotaging this attempt at legacy management, O'Neill uttered his most famous and most notorious sound-bite in May 1969:

It is frightfully hard to explain to protestants that if you give Roman Catholics a good job and a good house, they will live like protestants because they will see neighbours with cars and television sets; they will refuse to have eighteen children. But if a Roman Catholic is jobless, and lives in the most ghastly hovel, he will rear eighteen children on National Assistance. If you treat Roman Catholics with due consideration and kindness, they will live like protestants in spite of the authoritative nature of their Church.[3]

O'Neill had been trying to explain that protestants were wrong to think of catholics as hopeless social reprobates. But the condescension implicit in and essential to O'Neillism was made embarrassingly clear. Nor had O'Neill simply misspoken. He repeated exactly the same sentiments in a letter to his old friend, Jock Colville, the following month:

Housing discrimination was breaking down and in many of the new estates catholics and protestants were living side by side. The catholics, astonished by the prosperity, thrift and hard work of their protestant neighbours, defied their priests and refused to have fourteen children.[4]

O'Neill, despite his hopes, would not be remembered by catholics as their lost champion. They respected him, as they might, as more open-minded than his unionist brethren, but they knew he thought little of them. Conn McCluskey, with his wife Patricia a founder of the first civil rights organisation, the Campaign for Social Justice, wrote in an admittedly bitter memoir of how 'I have always felt hurt when the impression surfaces, as it often does, from time to time, that many protestants, deep down, regard us catholics as non-persons.' He gave as an example:

> Some years ago, after he resigned, Patricia and I travelled down alone in a lift at a hotel in London's Knightsbridge with Captain Terence O'Neill. He did not show even the slightest sign of recognition of two people who should surely have given him many times 'furiously to think.'[5]

As it happened, O'Neill's judgement as to the root of catholic alienation was not too dissimilar to McCluskey's, as he told an audience in 1977:

> Just as the WASPs in America have for so long – until recently – dominated the scene, so in Northern Ireland the protestants have ruled the roost. Sometimes people in the North say to me, 'Tell me Terence, what is it that the catholics haven't got?' I always reply, 'First class citizenship.' No reform can alter an attitude of mind, but I fear that so long as the majority regard the minority with disfavour and distaste, there will be plenty of dry tinder lying about, which can be ignited to start another explosion at some future date.[6]

O'Neill realised that legislation alone would not of itself overcome nationalist alienation.

AFTER STORMONT

O'Neill did not stay in Stormont long after his resignation. The serious violence of August 1969 and the introduction of British troops convinced him that its days were numbered: 'I really do not see how it can work any longer.'[7] He resigned his Stormont seat in January 1970, whereupon he was elevated to a life peerage as Baron O'Neill of the Maine. In a piercing blow, Paisley won O'Neill's Bannside seat in the following by-election (and when ultimately Paisley was appointed to the House of Lords in 2010, he took the title Baron Bannside). Though the cross-roads election marked the definitive end of aristocratic politics in Northern Ireland, many of those bourgeois who had rallied around O'Neill and the 'New Ulster Movement' in the '69 Crossroads election formed the Alliance Party of Northern Ireland in April 1970. Phelim O'Neill was its first leader, but Terence remained aloof. The Alliance Party was doggedly moderate and recognisably O'Neillite, but its support remained limited to a middle class five to ten per cent of so of the electorate.

O'Neill was studiedly moderate in the House of Lords, rejecting the New Right of Thatcherism.[8] His presidential, anti-party instincts remained, and in the early seventies he favoured a National Government and at one point even a 'British De Gaulle' to deal with the perceived crisis of governability.[9] For the United Kingdom in general, he still favoured devolution, as he told the Edinburgh University Union in May 1970:

> It is ludicrous that a Parliament [at Westminster] originally conceived for a few English farmers should today wrestle with the affairs of over fifty million people. The local affairs of Scotland should be dealt with in Scotland.[10]

This historic problem in Ireland he averred, perhaps mindful of his being let down by Queen Elizabeth II in 1966, was the monarchy's failures:

> No one played a greater role in precipitating the Irish crisis than Queen Victoria who hated Ireland and the Irish and refused to go there and allow the Prince of Wales to have a house there – in direct opposition to her attitude over Scotland which she loved and frequently visited.[11]

O'Neill no longer played any direct role in Unionist politics, though in 1971 he had to be put forward by his Party to debate with John Hume on French television, being the only politician they had able to speak French. Hume dominated the discussion, while O'Neill, sunk in an armchair, gave the impression of 'deep pessimism and lethargy'.[12]

O'Neill was if anything more involved in southern Irish affairs. In April 1972, after secret negotiations, he was appointed by the Irish government to the Board of Guardians of the National Gallery of Ireland for a five year term.[13] He frequently travelled south of the border on Gallery business, where he would stay at Malahide Castle with the aristocratic Talbots. More extraordinarily, in 1971 and 1972 O'Neill publicly entertained the thought of accepting nomination as next President of Ireland. No such nomination was forthcoming, and reactions to the idea, as the press noted, 'ranged from guffaws to anger'.[14]

AUTOBIOGRAPHY

In 1972, O'Neill published his autobiography. It was serialised in the *Sunday Press* and ran to its third-printing within five weeks, though the impression was that it sold better in the south of

Ireland than in the north.[15] This was a curious work. O'Neill had written it by hand, relying on memory, in exercise books on aeroplane flights back and forth between Northern Ireland and Great Britain. The result was a disjointed and anecdotal mishmash. Trips abroad and inconsequential encounters with the global rich and powerful featured prominently. The gaps were striking: there was no mention at all of the Pottinger Speech that set him on course for the Premiership; the Matthew Plan which laid the basis for his 'Changing the Face of Ulster'; the Civic Weeks and PEP that were his most developed articulation of 'bridge-building'; or of his support for pro-O'Neill independent candidates in the February 1969 crossroads election, his most audacious attempt to break the mould of Ulster politics. Name-dropping, peevish and sometimes snide, it was not a book that did his historical reputation much credit.

In pre-publication excerpts released to the press, O'Neill had included a pointed joke at Lord Brookeborough's expense: 'He was good company and a good raconteur, and those who met him imagined that he was relaxing away from his desk. However they did not realise that there was no desk.'[16] The Unionist Party was outraged at this jibe. Worse was to come when the book appeared. O'Neill's loyalty to his party, even to the Ulster protestant community at large, had all but disappeared. His opponents were invariably described as blinkered 'extremists', their abilities and sophistication continually depreciated, and private concerns expressed to him by his 'friends in the Unionist Party' were scornfully dismissed as 'the language of the master race.'[17] Has any other British political leader ever likened their followers to the Nazis? The shocked hurt and sense that their confidence had been betrayed never left his party. O'Neill was ever after a Unionist persona non grata.

NORTHERN IRELAND IN CRISIS

Politics moved at lightning speed in O'Neill's absence. When in August 1969 the British Army deployed onto the streets of Northern Ireland, it had become starkly evident Stormont was no longer the bulwark it had appeared against nationalist subversion and British treachery. The 1949 Ireland Act placing Northern Ireland's fate in the hands of Stormont was a dead letter. The old priority of pan-protestant unity to keep a grip on Stormont was now outdated, and pan-unionist solidarity cracked. Bill Craig's Vanguard organisation, established in February 1972, argued for the proto-sovereign legitimacy of Stormont, and more than dabbled with the idea of establishing an Independent Northern Ireland. Always rather unstable, Craig appeared to many as a potentially fascist leader, willing to lead a war to the knife against the violently resurgent IRA and its sympathisers. Faulkner, the great manoeuvrer, secured the leadership of the Ulster Unionist Party and Stormont's devolved government in March 1971, in a direct competition with Craig. Having finally fulfilled his personal (and family) ambition, Faulkner went on to offer more substantial reform to catholics and nationalists than had ever been countenanced by O'Neill. His introduction of internment without trial in August 1971, however, completed catholic alienation from Unionist government and massively increased violence on the streets. Faulkner lost any traction with the nationalist political opposition. When Stormont was prorogued in March 1972, he faced the real possibility that Craig would lead a protestant rebellion against Britain's direct-rule. In an episode of high drama, on 20 March 1972 Faulkner intervened to prevent Craig from declaring a provisional Ulster government before a huge protestant crowd from the balcony of Stormont parliament buildings, and he forced Craig to accept his supremacy, if temporarily.

Paisley, meanwhile, established in September 1970 the first serious loyalist political party opposed to the Ulster Unionist Party, the Democratic Unionist Party, a vehicle for his extraordinarily charismatic leadership and forceful rejection of compromise. Faulkner, endlessly buffeted but determined to win political mastery in the new dispensation, painfully negotiated the Sunningdale Agreement of 1973. This involved a power-sharing devolved government with the Social Democratic and Labour Party (SDLP) – a party sprung from the revolution in nationalist representation wrought by O'Neill's '69 'crossroads election' – and a cross-border 'Council of Ireland' with the Irish Government successors to Lemass. Faulkner's triumph, however, saw him humiliatingly rejected by Unionism; the erstwhile champion of 'party unity' was hounded from his own party. By twist of fate, Faulkner's new (and short-lived) Unionist Party of Northern Ireland was mostly comprised of those ex-O'Neill partisans who had not yet decamped to the Alliance Party. Sunningdale was destroyed by a general strike in May 1974 led by a coalition of Craig, Paisley, mainstream Unionists, and loyalist paramilitaries. Faulkner's well-earned reputation for unprincipled ambition and double-dealing, a legacy of his long undermining of O'Neill, helped destroy his greatest achievement.

THE END OF O'NEILLISM

Looking back, O'Neill never abandoned his class-based explanation of what had gone wrong for Northern Ireland. He shared (and had perhaps influenced) the famous 'Cameron interpretation' set-out in the report he had commissioned, that civil rights became an issue because a new generation of catholic middle-class leaders, benefitting from post-war access to grammar school education, had moved from traditional and 'backward' anti-partitionism to demanding 'British rights for British citizens'.[18] The fierce anti-unionism of Ulster's catholics and their determination to be recognised as both modern and fully Irish in the land of their birth, whilst never quite a closed book to O'Neill, was never fully acknowledged by him either. His gentry intuition only really extended as far as respect for bourgeois conformism. O'Neill saw remnants of the middle class moderation he had fostered as underpinning the 1973 power-sharing agreement. He had advised his 'friends' in the Irish government against insisting upon immediate establishment of the 'Council of Ireland'.[19]

When the Ulster Workers Council strike (and continued republican intransigence and violence) brought the power-sharing executive crashing down, O'Neill echoed some of those in the British Labour establishment who wondered whether Britain's role was coming to an end. 'Moderate middle-class protestants and catholics . . . have been unable to carry the working classes with them,' O'Neill admitted. Perhaps now they should stand aside:

> Just because those coming from a middle class background failed is no reason to state that no one else can succeed. If extreme protestants and extreme catholics who will be drawn largely from working-class backgrounds can bring peace to the Province, then those of us who have failed should wish them well.

The extremists on both sides have one thing in common, O'Neill argued; they are both 'largely anti-British'. Perhaps they could agree to take Ulster outside the United Kingdom, and from there negotiate a new relationship within Ireland?[20]

O'Neill's speculation was not realised in the 1970s, though it would have renewed relevance in the 1990s and early twenty-first century. As unionism re-stabilised after Sunningdale, with the remaining O'Neillites and Faulknerites shoved to the margins, direct rule from London clearly emerged as the popular protestant preference to a power-sharing Stormont. Increasingly desperate to revive his vision of Ulster self-rule, Craig in 1976 offered to the moderate nationalist SDLP an 'emergency' power-sharing government, only to be let-down and repudiated by Paisley. As Craig followed O'Neill and Faulkner into political oblivion, Paisley bid for supremacy in a unionist-controlled Northern Ireland by calling a political general strike in 1977. It was put down by the British government as a de facto attempted coup.[21] With its failure, unionism relapsed into stasis, opposing to any substantial reform or innovation. It would never again win the initiative.

When Faulkner, who had recently joined O'Neill in the House of Lords, was killed in a riding accident on 3 March, 1977, O'Neill's tribute was poignant, though he obviously still bore the scars:

> People in Northern Ireland know that Brian Faulkner and I rather parted company a few years ago; but it was one of the happier events in my life that when he took his seat last week I had a reunion with both Brian and his wife, Lucy, and I am very happy that this should have been so. . . . I feel that among the minority he may perhaps be recalled as the man who was the architect of internment. I hope that they will try, at this time, to forget that and to remember that this was the man who risked his political life and his political future in trying to establish a power-sharing Government. It is a tragedy that this has happened; although knowing Brian as I did and knowing that the hunting field was perhaps more important to him than anything else, I think that he probably would have been happier to end his life in this way than in ways which are so often open to people in Northern Ireland.[22]

O'Neill, meanwhile, busied himself with the Winston Churchill Memorial Trust, which allocated international travelling fellowships for young people. No doubt he sympathised with those who wanted to escape from the narrow horizons of their own communities. He now lived more or less permanently at Lymington Court in England, and had less and less to say about Northern Ireland. Mostly he involved himself in supporting adoption of a system of proportional representation for United Kingdom elections.

By the 1980s, a unionist division of labour had emerged, Paisley threatening Britain with tumult should London waver on the Union, whilst James Molyneaux's Ulster Unionists attempted to act as Number 10's candid friend. The aim was the same: obstruction. The Hunger Strikes of 1981, however, provided stark evidence that simple containment of militant Irish nationalism was not sustainable. Sinn Féin, illegal in O'Neill's time, now emerged as a major republican challenger to the SDLP for catholic votes. O'Neill by now had retired into obscurity. An academic and Irish Senator, Professor John A. Murphy, met him occasionally at the British-Irish Association, a discussion group centred on the problems of Northern Ireland. He found O'Neill's interest in Northern Ireland 'tempered by a certain melancholy, a certain depression, and a lack of any real hope about progress.'[23]

On 13 June 1990, O'Neill died of cancer at his home in Hampshire. He was 75. Only the previous day, the IRA had exploded a bomb in the same English county, at the former home of the leading Conservative figure Lord McAlpine. Responding to O'Neill's death, John Hume said that the North could have been saved great pain if only Unionists had followed his lead. Ian Paisley's verdict was that he had brought Northern Ireland from 'rock solid stability' into 'the turmoil of the civil rights movement.' The acrimony of the Northern Ireland conflict, both literal and rhetorical, had followed O'Neill to his last rest.

Signs of change were abroad, however. Five days after O'Neill was laid to rest, Gerry Adams intimated that it 'may not always be the case' that circumstances would 'permit' the IRA's 'right' of armed struggle.[24] Protracted negotiations led to IRA ceasefires in 1994 and 1997. The protestant electorate, aware that their veto on political change had evaporated, nominated the Ulster Unionists under David Trimble (formerly a Craig acolyte) to negotiate with the SDLP the 1998 Good Friday Agreement, and subsequently selected Paisley's DUP, from 2007, to operate with Sinn Féin a devolved government with a cross-border Irish dimension. Peace returned to Northern Ireland, more or less, and unionist domination was gone forever. But O'Neill's vision of a 'united Ulster' remained a distant prospect. He was far from forgotten, but his memory belonged to another age, one now barely visible from across the grim years during which, as he had warned, the tombstones were laid.

Notes

Chapter 1: *The Making of the Politician*

1   *The Unionist*, Sept. 1966.

2   *Hansard*, Parliamentary Debates: House of Lords, vol. 337, col. 189 (5 Dec. 1972).

3   Lord O'Neill of the Maine, *The Autobiography of Terence O'Neill: Prime Minister of Terence O'Neill 1963–1969* (London, 1972), pp 1–5.

4   'Captain the Rt. Hon. Terence Marne O'Neill, D. L., MP', Government of Northern Ireland Reference Library, PRONI.

5   O'Neill, *Autobiography*, p. 18.

6   Ibid, p. 8–9.

7   Ibid., p. 13.

8   Ibid, p. 14.

9   Terence O'Neill, 'A spectator's notebook', *Spectator*, 22 June 1974; 'One crowded hour', *Sunday Express*, 21 Jan. 1964.

10   O'Neill, *Autobiography*, p. 17

11   Ibid., pp 17–18.

12   'Premier's sights were once set on Westminster', *News Letter*, 22 Jan. 1968.

13   Desmond J. L. Fitzgerald, *History of the Irish Guards in the Second World War* (Aldershot, 1949), p. 366.

14   John Colville, *The Fringes of Power: Downing Street Diaries 1939–55* (London, 1985), pp 499–500.

15   Fitzgerald, *Irish Guards*, p. 426.

16   'A fighting Irish O'Neill goes back to a memory that will never fade', *Daily Express*, 3 Sept. 1964.

17   'O'Neill's well-loved in village', *News Letter*, 27 Mar. 1963.

18   Martin Wallace, 'Profile: Terence O'Neill', *Belfast Telegraph* (hereafter *BT*), 19 May 1961.

19 F. S. L. Lyons , *Culture and Anarchy in Ireland 1890–1939* (Oxford, 1979), p. 113.

20 'O'Neill looks back through rose tinted spectacles', *Irish Times*, 8 Nov. 1972.

21 'Dad was stabbed in back: Anne O'Neill', *BT*, 25 Apr. 1969.

22 Brian Faulkner, *Memoirs of a Statesman* (London, 1978), p. 14.

23 James Kelly, 'Terence joins the lordly brigade', *Sunday Independent*, 4 Jan. 1970.

24 'Premier's sights were once set on Westminster', 22 Jan. 1968.

25 *Daily Express*, 27 Jan. 1970.

26 Then in the throes of civil war between Communists and monarchists.

27 M. Chapman-Walker, 'Confidential report', 19 Feb. 1951, Conservative Party Archive, Bodleian Library, Oxford, CCO2/2/21, p. 1.

28 David Bleakley in *News Letter*, 15 Nov. 1963.

29 See 'Salaries etc. of ministers and Members of Parliament', cabinet conclusions, 28 Nov. 1963, CAB/4/1246/10.

30 Nancy Kinghan, *United We Stood: The Official History of the Ulster Women's Unionist Council 1911–1974* (Belfast, 1975), p. 79.

31 Terence O'Neill, 'Ulster: the communication gap', *The Spectator*, 15 June 1974.

32 Henry Patterson and Eric Kaufman, *Unionism and Orangeism in Northern Ireland Since 1945: The Decline of the Loyal Family* (Manchester, 2007), p. 65.

33 Jonathan Bardon, *A History of Ulster* (Belfast, 1992), pp 593–6, 609.

34 O'Neill, *Autobiography*, p. 47.

35 *Hansard*, Parliamentary Debates: House of Lords, vol. 355, col. 1222 (12 Dec. 1974).

36 'Unionists back new Prime Minister', *BT*, 26 Mar. 1963.

37 Martin Wallace, 'Profile', *BT*, 19 May 1961.

38 John Cole, 'Ulster's last chance', *The Guardian*, 9 Nov. 1972.

39 'Northern Ireland Annual Review 1956', *News Letter*, 4 Jan. 1957, p. 19.

40 Transcript of interview with Lord O'Neill for 'This week–five long years', July 1974.

41 'O'Neill defends Claridges bash', *News Letter*, 8 June 1964.

42 'The agony and the anarchy', *Daily Mail*, 31 Jan. 1969.

43 'A passion for politics', *The Guardian*, 9 Nov. 1974.

44 *Hansard*, Northern Ireland House of Commons (hereafter NIHC), vol. 49, cc 757–8 (8 Nov. 1961).

45 Kenneth Bloomfield, *Stormont in Crisis* (Belfast, 1994), p. 28; John Cole, 'Introduction', in Terence O'Neill, *Ulster at the Crossroads* (London, 1969), p. 21.

46 Martin Wallace, 'Profile', *BT*, 19 May 1961.

47 'Northern Ireland's new Prime Minister', *Irish Times*, 30 Mar. 1963.

48 O'Neill, *Autobiography*, pp 35, 38, 58, 62–3.

49 'Personal note from the Minister of Finance', n.d. [1958], papers of the Cabinet Employment Committee, PRONI, CAB/4A/38/29.

50 David Gordon, *The O'Neill Years* (Belfast, 1989), p 9.

51 NIHC, vol. 44, c. 1569 (21 May 1959).

52 Henry Kennedy, 'Politics in Northern Ireland: a study in one-party domination', unpublished PhD, University of Michigan, 1967, footnote, p. 59.

53 For example, NIHC, vol. 44, c. 1506 (20 May 1959).

54 Andrew Gailey, *Crying in the Wilderness* (Belfast, 1995), p 58.

55 Faulkner, *Memoirs of a Statesman*, p 17.

Chapter 2: *Into the Premiership*

1   K. S. Isles and Norman Cuthbert, *An Economic Survey of Northern Ireland* (Belfast, 1957), p. 350.

2   Ibid, pp 189–90, 349.

3   Paul Bew, Peter Gibbon and Henry Patterson, *The State in Northern Ireland* (London, 1995), p. 128; Belinda Probert, *Beyond Orange and Green: The Political Economy of the Northern Ireland Crisis* (London, 1978), p. 80.

4   Michael Moss and John R. Hume, *Shipbuilders to the World: 125: Years of Harland and Wolff* (Belfast, 1986), p. 383.

5   Ibid., p 391.

6   'Memorandum by the Secretary of State', National Archives, Kew, HO284/61, p. 4. See also R. A. B. Butler, 'Memorandum to the Secretary of State', ibid.

7   'Draft paper for Economic Policy Committee; unemployment policy in Northern Ireland, memorandum by the Home Secretary', ibid.

8   Derek Birrell and Alan Murie, *Policy and Government in Northern Ireland* (Dublin, 1980), pp 15–8.

9   Arthur J. Green, *Devolution and Public Finances: Stormont from 1921 to 1972* (Strathclyde, 1979), p. 14.

10 Birrell and Murie, *Policy and Government*, p. 17, p. 20.

11 Harold Evans, *Downing Street Diaries: The Macmillan Years 1957–1963* (London, 1981), pp 128–9.

12 Cabinet conclusions, 7 Mar. 1961, National Archives, Kew, CAB 128; 'Unemployment in Northern Ireland, memorandum by the Secretary of State for the Home Department', National Archives, Kew, CAB 129/104.

13 *New Statesman*, Oct. 1958.

14 'Report by officials on the proposals by the Northern Ireland Government for the relief of unemployment in Northern Ireland', no date (May 1961) in 'Hall Report', National Archives, Kew, HO284/63.

15 R. J. Lawrence, *The Government of Northern Ireland: Public Finance and Public Services* (Oxford, 1965), p. 101.

16 Report of the joint working party on the economy of Northern Ireland, CMD 446 (Belfast, 1962).

17 Ibid., para. 17.

18 Tom Wilson, *Ulster: Conflict and Consent* (Oxford, 1989), p. 88.

19 *The Round Table: The Commonwealth Journal of International Affairs* (1962), pp 282–3.

20 Bew, Gibbon and Patterson, *Northern Ireland*, pp 124–34.

21 Terence O'Neill, *Ulster at the Crossroads* (London, 1969), pp 31–4.

22 Ibid., p. 31.

23 Arthur J. Green, *Devolution and Public Finances: Stormont from 1921 to 1972* (Strathclyde, 1979), p. 17.

24 J. A. Oliver, *Working at Stormont* (Dublin, 1978), p. 82.

25 Ibid., p 86.

26 'Change of Prime Minister: March 1963', National Archives, Kew, HO284/57, p. 1.

27 Lord O'Neill of the Maine, *The Autobiography of Terence O'Neill: Prime Minister of Terence O'Neill 1963–1969* (London, 1972), pp 40–3.

28 Andrew Boyd, *Brian Faulkner and the Crisis of Ulster Unionism* (Tralee, 1972), pp 55–6.

29 'Change of Prime Minister: March 1963', pp 2–3.

30 James Kelly, 'Cloak-and-dagger tactics behind the Unionist crisis', *Sunday Independent*, 25 Sept. 1965.

31 'Change of Prime Minister: March 1963: supplementary note', HO284/57. See also Minutes of a Parliamentary Unionist Party meeting, 1953, cited by Warnock in 'MPs had no choice on Prime Minister: Warnock', *BT*, 24 Oct. 1963.

32 'Criticism of method of choice of Prime Minister', *BT*, 23 Oct. 1963.

33 *BT*, 30 Apr. 1963.

34 James Boswell, *The Life of Samuel Johnson*, vol. 2 (London, 1949), p. 291.

35 'Our special correspondent in the republic', *BT*, 16 July 1963.

36 'Councillor to fight "no Kennedy Road plan"', *BT*, 21 Jan. 1964; 'No more on JFK road name protest', ibid., 4 Feb. 1964; '"Kennedy Drive" discussion tonight', *News Letter*, 3 Feb. 1964.

37 Timothy Patrick Coogan, *Ireland since the Rising* (Connecticut, 1966), p. 316.

38 O'Neill Diary, O'Neill Papers (14 Oct. 1963).

39 See comments of Ivan Neill, 'Northern Ireland economic plan', Cabinet Conclusions, PRONI, CAB/4/1283/3, p. 1.

40 'Beatles vitality typical of Britain: O'Neill', *BT*, 13 Mar. 1964.

41 'Northern Ireland needs aggressive sales drive: PM', *BT*, 25 May 1964.

42 'Ulster is underused national asset, says Capt. O'Neill', *BT*, 12 Nov. 1964.

43 'O'Neill opens the Giant's Causeway', *News Letter*, 25 June 1963.

44 O'Neill, *Crossroads*, p. 41.

45 Ibid., p 15.

46 'Another example of centralising on Belfast', *BT*, 20 Nov., 1964.

47 Henry Benson, *Northern Ireland Railways* (Belfast, 1963) CMD 458.

48 Economic plan for Northern Ireland (non-agenda item)', Cabinet Conclusions, 21 Oct. 1963, PRONI, CAB/4/1239/11, pp 4–5.

49 Ibid., p 5.

50 *BT*, 16 Jan. 1964.

51 'Labour "thunder" stolen', *News Letter*, 23 Oct. 1963.

52 O'Neill, *Autobiography*, p. 52.

53 Warnock, 'Why recognition is withheld', *News Letter*, 22 Aug. 1963.

54 'Faulkner: Cabinet conclusions', 11 Mar. 1964, PRONI, CAB/4/1259/11. Craig told the trade unionists to go 'take a running jump' in 1963. *Belfast Telegraph*, 1 June 1963.

55 *The Unionist*, Feb. 1965.

56 HL Debates, vol. 378, cc 137–270 (30 Nov. 1976).

57 'Diary written on flight from Detroit to Minneapolis, North America Sept./Oct. 1963', 12 Oct., O'Neill Papers.

58 'I disclaim any link with city plans: Copcutt', *BT*, 10 Dec. 1964.

59 Cabinet Conclusions, 9 Apr. 1964, PRONI, CAB/4/1261/7, p. 4.

60 'Planners keep list of names', *BT*, 10 Dec. 1964.

61 'New city: formal steps', Cabinet Conclusions, 6 July 1965, PRONI, CAB/4/1312/17, pp 3–4.

62 NIHC, vol. 61, c. 1494 (6 July 1965).

63 Editorial, 'Rename this child', *BT*, 7 July 1965.

64 Henry Patterson and Eric Kaufman, *Unionism and Orangeism in Northern Ireland since 1945: The Decline of the Loyal Family* (Manchester, 2007), pp 67–8.

65 *News Letter*, 2 Sept. 1963.

66 New City Design Group, 'First report on the proposed new city' (Belfast, 1964), p. 50; 'Craigavon new city, second report on the plan' (Belfast, 1967), p. 51.

67 Tim Blackman, 'Craigavon: the development and dismantling of Northern Ireland's new town', *Capital and Class*, no. 35 (London, 1987), pp 123–4.

68 'Coleraine may be centre of "exciting" developments', *BT*, 10 Feb. 1965.

69 'Thousands asked to join university protest motorcade', *BT*, 12 Feb. 1965.

70 'Derry appeal for all in sympathy to join motorcade', *BT*, 15 Feb. 1965.

71 'Mayor presents city's claim', *BT*, 18 Feb. 1965.

72 'Derry sold down the river: Nixon' and 'MP's political future in doubt', *BT*, 8 May 1965.

73 NIHC, vol. 61, c. 423 (26 May 1965). For profiles of the seven accused, *The Londonderry Sentinel*, 2 June 1965.

74 'Dr. Nixon to remain North Down MP', *BT*, 5 June 1965.

75 'Dissolution: Nov. 5 …', *BT*, 27 Oct., 1965.

76 Ron Wiener, *The Rape and Plunder of the Shankill* (Belfast, 1976), pp 52–69. Liam O'Dowd, 'Regional policy', in Liam O'Dowd, Bill Rolston and Mike Tomilson (eds), *Northern Ireland: Between Civil Rights and Civil War* (London, 1980), p. 39.

77 Blackman, 'Craigavon', p. 127.

78 Frank Gallager, 'Cleavages and consensus: Craigavon Borough Council, 1973–81', unpublished MSc thesis (Belfast, 1983), p. 1.

79 Government of Northern Ireland Economic Section, Northern Ireland Economic Report on 1969 (Belfast, 1970), p. 8.

80 'Meeting at Downing Street on 4th Nov., 1968', CAB/4/1413/9.

81 Richard I. D. Harris, *Regional Economic Policy in Northern Ireland, 1945–1988* (Aldershot, 2008), p. 33, p. 52.

Chapter 3: *O'Neillism and Paisleyism*

1 *BT*, 17 Sept.–15 Oct. 1962; 'Which foot do you dig with' (book review), *The Spectator*, 18 Jan. 1963.

2 Denis P. Barritt and Charles F. Carter, *The Northern Ireland Problem: A Study in Group Relations*, 2nd edn (Oxford, 1972), pp 126–7.

3 'RUC out in force on Falls Road', *News Letter*, 18 June 1963.

4 *News Letter*, 30 Mar. 1964.

5 They had been up since 6 Sept. without being noticed.

6 'Minister may restrict march by Paisley supporters', *BT*, 28 Sept. 1964.

7 'Tricolour protest rally to go on at City Hall', *BT*, 29 Sept. 1964.

8 *BT*, 1 Oct. 1964; 'More violence in West Belfast', *Irish Times*, 3 Oct. 1964.

9 Denis Barritt, *Northern Ireland: A Problem to Every Solution* (London, 1982), pp 6–7.

10 'PM's visit to catholic school in Ballymoney', *Irish News*, 25 Apr. 1964.

11 'Captain Terence O'Neill talks to the Mail', *Daily Mail*, undated Press cutting, Linen Hall Library, Political Colletion, Belfast, 1965.

12 'Unionist executive approves Prime Ministers' talks', *BT*, 23 Jan. 1965.

13 'Finding a basis for North-South co-operation', *New Ireland* society, 1964.

14 'Faulkner ready to talk trade if Éire makes it worthwhile', *BT*, 15 Dec. 1965.

15 Press cutting, *Sunday Telegraph*, 17 Jan. 1965, 'Meeting of Taoiseach and Prime Minister of Northern Ireland', 305/14/361 IA.

16 'News of talks a political bombshell in Dublin', *BT*, 14 Jan. 1965.

17 Barry White, 'The day Lemass came to Stormont', *Belfast Telegraph*, n.d. [1975]; 'PM and THAT meeting', *BT*, 5 Feb. 1965.

18 'O'Neill tells of "secret agent" behind talks', *BT*, 4 Feb. 1965. Tony Gray, *The Irish Answer: An Anatomy of Modern Ireland* (London, 1966), p. 380.

19 Gray, *The Irish answer*, p. 380.

20 Terence O'Neill, 'A spectator's notebook', *Spectator*, 22 June 1974.

21 Lord O'Neill of the Maine, *The Autobiography of Terence O'Neill: Prime Minister of Terence O'Neill 1963–1969* (London, 1972), p. 72.

22 W. H. Van Voris, *Violence in Ulster: An Oral Documentary* (Amherst, 1975), p. 41.

23 'Mr Paisley takes protest letter to PM', *BT*, 15 Jan. 1965.

24 'Protest petition', *BT*, 15 Jan. 1965.

25 'Cross denominational barriers', *BT*, 20 Feb. 1968.

26 'Resolution adopted on official opposition', Nationalist Party Archive, PRONI, D/2994/3/3/11.

27 'MP urges better cross-border feeling', *BT*, 27 Jan., 1965.

28 'Wives join Ulster and Éire leaders at lunch', *BT*, 9 Feb. 1965.

29 'Remarkable claims by Mrs Seán Lemass', *Sunday People*, 4 Nov. 1973.

30 Memo from Commonwealth Secretary to Wilson, 22 July 1965, National Archives, Kew, PREM/13/983.

31 *BT*, 8 Dec. 1967.

32 'Unity not likely in my lifetime', *Irish News*, 9 Nov. 1972.

33 'No concessions sought by rebels', *BT*, 28 Sept. 1966.

34 Editorial, 'Standing up to it', *BT*, 9 Mar. 1966.

35 *BT*, 7 Apr. 1966.

36 'Lord O'Neill blames protestants', *Irish Independent*, 8 Nov. 1972.

37 'Police will go all out to catch bomb men' and 'Widow burned by petrol bombs', *BT*, 9 May 1966.

38 'We wage war on IRA: statement', *BT*, 21 May 1966.

39 'Stabbed man to be exhumed', *BT*, 22 June 1966.

40 'Prime Minister flying back from Paris', *BT*, 27 June 1966.

41 NIHC, vol. 64, 29 June 1966.

42 Margaret O'Callaghan and Catherine O'Donnell, 'The Northern Ireland Government, the "Paisleyite Movement" and Ulster Unionism in 1966', in *Irish Political Studies*, vol. 12, no. 2 (2006).

43 'General Assembly will discuss aid to Mater', *BT*, 4 June 1966.

44 '200 bar way to Paisley march' and 'Rioters clash with protestant march', *BT*, 7 June 1966.

45 NIHC, vol. 64, c. 331 (15 June, 1966).

46 Ibid., c. 327.

47 *Irish Times*, 22 Feb. 1966; Memorandum, 18 Feb. 1966, 'Northern Ireland; royal matters: general', PRONI, HO5/149.

48 '"Yes" to Queen Bridge: after a storm', *BT*, 1 Mar. 1966.

49 'Carson visits father's statue', *BT*, 1 Mar. 1966.

50 'Unionists gear to Carson challenge', *BT*, 10 Mar. 1966.

51 *Irish Times*, 5 July 1966. *BT*, 4 July 1966.

52 Terence O'Neill, 'The Queen's visit', July 1966, O'Neill Papers.

53 'Seven are charged with unlawful assembly', *BT*, 18 July 1966.

54 'Pubs looted' and 'Incident after Paisley parade', *BT*, 23 July 1966.

55 *BT*, 26 July 1966.

56 As recalled later. Minutes of the Parliamentary Unionist Party, 12 Dec. 1968, p. 2. Linen Hall Library, Belfast.

57 James Kelly, 'Cloak-and-dagger tactics behind Unionist crisis', *Sunday Independent*, 25 Sept. 1966.

58 *BT*, 24 June 1966.

59 Ibid., 11 Feb. 1969.

60 *The Unionist*, Oct. 1966.

61 Minutes of the Parliamentary Unionist Party, 12 Dec. 1968, Linen Hall Library.

62 *Daily Telegraph*, 9 Nov. 1972, press cuttings, NIO files, Linen Hall Library.

63 Coralie Kinahan, *Behind Every Great Man …?* (Temple Patrick, n.d. [1997]), p. 303.

64 Van Voris, *Violence in Ulster*, p. 42.

65 '"A conspiracy," says PM', *BT*, 24 Sept. 1966.

66 *BT*, 26 Sept. 1966.

67 Brian Faulkner, *Memoirs of a Statesman* (London, 1978), p. 40.

68 *BT*, 28, 29 Sept. 1966.

69 Letter to Terence O'Neill, 29 Sept. 1966, Papers of Peter Montgomery, PRONI, D627/A/2/193.

70 *BT*, 8 Oct. 1966.

71 Van Voris, *Violence in Ulster*, p. 45.

72 *BT*, 8 Oct. 1966.

73 Minutes of the Parliamentary Unionist Party, 26 June 1969, p. 1, Linen Hall Library.

74 *BT*, 27 Apr. 1967.

75 O'Neill, *Autobiography*, p. 86. Faulkner, *Memoirs of a Statesman*, p. 41.

76 David Bleakley, *Faulkner: Conflict and Consent* (Oxford, 1974), p 74.

77 Lord Brookeborough to Terence O'Neill, 31 May 1967, PRONI D3004/C/3.

78 Interview with Michael Mills, 'Removing the balance of hatred', *Irish Press*, 27 Mar. 1968.

Chapter 4: *O'Neill's PEP Pill*

1   'Ulster should lead attack on restrictive practices', *BT*, 15 Feb. 1965.

2   'Premier at protestant/catholic conference', *BT*, 9 Apr. 1966.

3   Editorial, 'Over the bridge', *BT*, 9 Apr. 1966.

4   'Warm welcome for Prime Minister's tolerance plea', *BT*, 9 Apr. 1966.

5   Westminster Commons debates, vol. 729, cc 721–3 (26 May 1966).

6   'Unionist delegates urged to avoid extreme "insularity"', *BT*, 30 Apr. 1966.

7   *BT*, 2 Nov. 1966.

8   Westminster Commons debates, vol. 729, cc 721–3 (26 May 1966).

9   'O'Neill is stalling on reforms Fitt says', *BT*, 19 June 1967.

10 'Discussions at Downing Street on 5th Aug., 1966', PRONI, CAB/4/1338/2.

11 'Premiers discuss Westminster: Stormont "difficulties"', *BT*, 5 Aug. 1966.

12 'Discussions at Downing Street, 5th Aug., 1966', Supplementary cabinet conclusions, 9 Aug. 1966, PRONI, CAB/4/1338/3.

13 'Opposition expect faster reform', *BT*, 6 Aug. 1966.

14 'Premier strikes "self-reliance" keynote', *BT*, 23 Jan. 1967.

15 'Civic Weeks slump', *BT*, 17 Apr. 1969.

16 *BT*, 24 May 1967.

17 Ibid., 20 Feb. 1968.

18 'Memorandum by the Director of Information on 50th anniversary celebrations', CAB/4/1399/4.

19 'NILP warns O'Neill about "real danger"', *BT*, 24 June 1968.

20 'Preserve local centres: Prime Minister', *BT*, 27 Sept. 1968.

21 'Chanting students "squat" in street', *BT*, 9 Oct. 1968.

22 *BT*, 28 Mar. 1969.

23 'Civic weeks slump', *BT*, 17 Apr. 1969.

24 F. Cochrane, 'Meddling at the crossroads', in R. English and G. Walker, *Unionism in Modern Ireland* (Basingstoke, 1996), pp 149–50, p. 164.

25 NIHC, vol. 65, cc 4–10, 32–45 (13 Dec. 1966).

26 'Boundary commission report', *BT*, 16 Dec. 1966.

27 'Stormont statement ends seven month controversy', *BT*, 23 May 1968.

28 *Sunday Press*, 25 Sept. 1966.

29 Kenneth Bloomfield, *Stormont in Crisis* (Belfast, 1994), pp 99–100.

Chapter 5: *The North Explodes*

1   'Missiles and jeers from crowd', *BT*, 21 May 1968.

2   *BT*, 24 June 1968.

3   'Unionist walk-out as Currie speaks', *BT*, 25 July 1968.

4   'Protesters stop Derry council meeting', *BT*, 27 Aug. 1968.

5   'Report by three MPs accuse RUC men', *BT*, 10 Oct. 1968.

6   'Disturbances in Londonderry', Cabinet conclusions, 8 Oct. 1968, CAB/4/1405/10.

7   'Memorandum by the Prime Minister', 14 Oct. 1968, CAB/4/1406.

8   Ibid.

9   Fergus Pyle, 'Silent Unionists being heard', *Irish Times*, 29 Oct. 1968.

10 *BT*, 17 Feb. 1969.

11 'Meeting at Downing Street on 4th Nov., 1968', CAB/4/1413/9, p. 2.

12 Cabinet conclusions, 7 Nov. 1968, CAB/4/1413/22, p. 4.

13 Minutes of the Parliamentary Unionist Party, 12 Nov. 1968, Linen Hall Library, Belfast.

14 Max Hastings, *Ulster 1969* (London, 1970), p. 66.

15 Andrew Gailey, *Crying in the Wilderness* (Belfast, 1995), p 138.

16 Cabinet Conclusions, 20 Nov. 1968, CAB/4/1418/11, p. 2.

17 *BT*, 21 Nov. 1968.

18 Ibid., 23 Nov. 1968.

19 Cabinet conclusions, 19 Oct. 1968, CAB/4/1419, p. 3.

20 Minutes of the Parliamentary Unionist Party, 12 Dec. 1968, p. 6, Linen Hall Library.

21 Martin Wallace, *Drums, Guns and Revolution in Ulster* (London, 1970), p. 43.

22 NIHC, vol. 70, cc 2181–4 (4 Dec. 1968).

23 *BT*, 9 Dec. 1968.

24 W. H. Van Voris, *Violence in Ulster: An Oral Documentary* (Amherst, 1975), p. 45.

25 Terence O'Neill, *Ulster at the Crossroads* (London, 1969), pp 140–6.

26 *BT*, 16, 18 Dec. 1968. By way of indirect comparison, 25,500 signed a civil rights/human rights year petition in Derry alone on one day, 10 Dec. 1968; *BT*, 11 Dec. 1968.

27 *Daily Mail*, 31 Jan. 1969, press cuttings, O'Neill Papers.

28 'Election notebook: battle has split South Derry', *BT*, 7 Feb. 1969.

29 *BT*, 3 Feb. 1969.

30 Speeches and statements, Jan. 1969, PRONI, INF/3/3/92.

31 'Bradford hints at cut in student grants', *BT*, 10 Jan. 1969.

32 Ministry of Home Affairs Memorandum, 9 Jan. 1969, PRONI, HA/32/2/31.

33 'RUC insist on re-routing', *BT*, 11 Jan. 1969.

34 Cabinet minutes 10 Jan. 1969, PRONI, CAB/4/1425.

35 *BT*, 13 Jan. 1969.

36 *BT*, 17 Jan. 1969.

37 Cabinet conclusions, 15 Jan. 1969, CAB/4/1427.

38 'West calls it "high-handed"', *BT*, 16 Jan. 1969.

39 'Inquiry will grant rights: Hume', *BT*, 16 Jan. 1969.

40 Editorial, 'Quiet week-end', *BT*, 17 Jan. 1969.

41 For exchange of letters see: Lord O'Neill of the Maine, *The Autobiography of Terence O'Neill: Prime Minister of Terence O'Neill 196–1969* (London, 1972), pp 150–4.

42 'Election act of irresponsibility say rebel MPs', *BT*, 4 Feb. 1969.

43 Cabinet statement, 'Cabinet gives the reasons', ibid.

44 'Eggs, fruit thrown at O'Neill's car', *BT*, 29 Jan. 1969.

45 'O'Neill replies to "unity" criticism', *BT*, 7 Feb. 1968.

46 'Eggs, fruit thrown at O'Neill's car', op. cit.

47 Tony Geraghty, 'O'Neill wages geurilla war in own party', *Sunday Times*, 1969.

48 *BT*, 3 Feb. 1969.

49 'Movement launched to back premier', *BT*, 6 Feb. 1969.

50 13 Feb. 1969, Correspondence of Mary McNeill, Institute of Irish Studies.

51 Constituency profile, *BT*, 15 Feb. 1969.

52 *BT*, 14 Feb. 1969.

53 Barry White, 'A test of parties', *BT*, 13 Feb. 1969.

54 'Bailie warns dissidents', *BT*, 22 Feb. 1969.

55 'Boyle protest', *BT*, 12 Feb. 1969.

56 John Biggs-Davison, *The Cross of St Patrick: The Catholic Unionist Tradition in Ireland* (London, 1985), p. 377.

57 *BT*, 14 Feb. 1969.

58 13 Feb. 1969, Correspondence of Mary McNeill.

59 Burns interviewed in *BT*, 20 Feb. 1969.

60 *BT*, 3 Feb. 1969.

61 'Conversions staggering: Bradford', *BT*, 17 Feb. 1969.

62 *BT*, 19 Feb. 1969.

63 Ibid., 1 May 1969.

64 Ibid., 3 Feb. 1969.

65 'Premier goes all out', *News Letter*, 18 Feb. 1969.

66 Harold Jackson, 'O'Neill stands aloof from Craig's banter', *The Times*, 18 Feb. 1969.

67 'Destiny at stake: marquis', *BT*, 6 Feb. 1969.

68 'Duke to rally O'Neill forces', *BT*, 1 Feb. 1969.

69 'Catholics in west hold key votes', *BT*, 21 Feb. 1969.

70 'Anderson still wants change', *BT*, 18 Feb. 1969.

71 *BT*, 4, 21 Feb. 1969.

72 'Three optimistic men fight for the votes in East Down', *BT*, 22 Feb. 1969.

73 'Election notebook: class war must stop', *BT*, 13 Feb. 1969.

74 '"Split vote can cost me seat", Faulkner says', *BT*, 20 Feb. 1969.

75 'Prime Minister launches his party manifesto', *BT*, 14 Feb. 1969. Faulkner replied that he had only an eight acre holding. 'Craig says O'Neill "childish"', *BT*, 15 Feb. 1969.

76 'Question my opponents attitudes', *BT*, 21 Feb. 1969.

77 'I will not back any "rebels" - Prime Minister', *BT*, 20 Feb. 1969.

78 'Work together for Ulster: Prime Minister', *BT*, 22 Feb. 1969.

79 'Question my opponents' attitudes', ibid.

80 'Catholic doubts about O'Neill's appeal', *Irish Press*, 1 Mar. 1969.

81 Barry White, 'A test of parties', *BT*, 13 Feb. 1969.

82 Paul Compton, 'The Demographic Background', in David Watt (ed.), *The Constitution of Northern Ireland: Problems and Prospects* (London, 1981), p. 89

83 'Prime Minister back but so are his opponents', *BT*, 25 Feb. 1969.

84 *Washington Post*, 21 Jan. 1969.

85 R. S. P. Elliott and John Hickie, *Ulster: A Case Study in Conflict Theory* (London, 1971), p. 64.

86 Roy Lilley, 'Ready to fight on', *BT*, 25 Feb. 1969.

87 Minutes of the Parliamentary Unionist Party, 28 Feb. 1968, p. 2, Linen Hall Library.

88 Ibid., p. 1.

89 'Difficult for Prime Minister to last', *BT*, 26 Feb. 1969.

90 *BT*, 27 Mar. 1969.

91 'Prime Minister's bid to heal party wounds', *BT*, 31 Mar. 1969.

92 'Anti-O'Neill forces now aim at capturing executive', *BT*, 1 Apr. 1969.

93 *BT*, 6 May 1969.

94 T. Hennessy, *The Origins of the Troubles* (Dublin, 2005); S. Prince, *Northern Ireland's '68* (Dublin, 2007).

95 *News Letter*, 20 Feb. 1969.

96 *BT*, 8 Mar. 1969.

97 Ibid., 21 Apr. 1969.

98 O'Neill, *Autobiography*, p. 122.

99 Terence O'Neill, Diary of the last days, written 6–8 May 1969, O'Neill Papers.

100 Ibid.

101 Cabinet conclusions, 22 Apr. 1969, CAB/4/1437; *BT*, 22 Apr. 1969.

102 Minutes of the Parliamentary Unionist Party, 21 Apr. 1969, p. 1. Linen Hall Library.

103 Westminster Commons debates, vol. 782, c. 322 (22 Apr. 1969).

104 'Walkout after narrow vote for franchise reform', *BT*, 23 Apr. 1969. '"Timing" on vote brings shock move', *BT*, 24 Apr. 1969.

105 'Unionist struggle still on?', *BT*, 30 Jan. 1969.

106 'Pleased with backing of party leaders', *BT*, 31 Jan. 1969.

107 Minutes of the Parliamentary Unionist Party, 22 Apr. 1969, pp 4–5, Linen Hall Library.

108 O'Neill, Diary of the last days, O'Neill Papers.

109 John F. Harbinson, *The Ulster Unionist Party* (Belfast, 1973), p. 154.

110 Speeches and statements, Apr. 1969, PRONI, INF/3/3/95.

111 O'Neill, Diary of the last days, O'Neill Papers.

112 Ibid., *BT*, 29 Apr. 1969.

113 *BT*, 30 Apr. 1969.

Chapter 6: *Legacy*

1 Seán Mac Stíofáin, *Memoirs of a Revolutionary* (Edinburgh, 1975), p. 104.

2 'Ulster at the Crossroads', CAB9F/123/171, PRONI.

3 *BT*, 10 May 1969.

4 29 July 1969, O'Neill Papers.

5 Conn McCluskey, *Up off their Knees: A Commentary on the Civil Rights Movement in Northern Ireland* (Republic of Ireland, 1989), pp 6–7.

6 Speech to Leinster Society of Chartered Accountants, Dublin, 24 Nov. 1977, O'Neill Papers.

7 Letter to John Cole, 28 Apr. 1970, O'Neill Papers.

8   HL Debates, vol. 315, c. 405 (15 Feb. 1971); vol. 332, c. 1427 (5 July 1972); vol. 338, c. 917 (5 Feb. 1973); vol. 339, cc 902–3 (5 Mar. 1973); vol. 348, c. 375 (19 Dec. 1973); vol. 350, cc 69–70 (13 Mar. 1974); vol. 460, c. 70 (11 Feb. 1985).

9   Ibid., vol. 332, c. 1428 (5 July 1972); vol. 354, c. 118 (30 Oct. 1974).

10 Commission on the Constitution, HO221/161, p. 4.

11 Ibid., p. 5. Even the Scottish Nationalists love their Queen.

12 'The North on French TV', *Irish Press*, 23 Feb. 1971.

13 'Lord O'Neill appointment', *Sunday Independent*, 23 Apr. 1972.

14 'O'Neill for President', *Sunday Independent*, 26 Nov. 1972.

15 'Rebels always win, says O'Neill', *Irish News*, 1973.

16 Lord O'Neill of the Maine, *The Autobiography of Terence O'Neill: Prime Minister of Terence O'Neill 1963–1969* (London, 1972), p. 40.

17 Ibid., p. 87.

18 'Unionist blunders – by O'Neill', *Irish Press*, 19 Jan. 1974. *Disturbances in Northern Ireland* [Cameron Report] (Belfast, 1969), p. 15, para. 11.

19 'O'Neill plea to Dublin Government', *Irish Times*, 15 Mar. 1974.

20 Lord O'Neill, 'Can extremists unite?', *The Observer*, 7 Apr. 1974.

21 Roy Mason, *Paying the Price* (London, 1999), pp 173–98.

22 HL Debates, vol. 380, cc 829–35 (3 Mar. 1977).

23 Seanad Éireann debates, vol. 125, 14 June, 1990.

24 Interview with Gerry Adams, *Sunday Tribune*, 1990.

Select Bibliography

Terence O'Neill's *Autobiography* (London, 1972) is, as I discuss in the main text, rather unfair to O'Neill's strengths and achievements. Obviously drier, but in many respects more useful, is the collection of his speeches and statements, *Ulster at the Crossroads (London, 1969)*. Brian Faulkner's *Memoirs of a Statesman (London, 1978)* gives the view of O'Neill's chief nemesis. Vignettes of O'Neill's war career can be found in Desmond J. L. Fitzgerald, *History of the Irish Guards in the Second World War* (Aldershot, 1949). As this book was based upon information provided by Intelligence Officers, O'Neill probably had a direct hand in its composition. A short memoir by the Unionist minister Ivan Neill, *Church and State* (Dunmurray, 1995) has interesting material particularly for the 1950s and early 1960s. Kenneth Bloomfield was a senior civil servant in the 1960s and O'Neill's speech-writer. His *Stormont in Crisis* (Belfast, 1994) gives an inside view from O'Neill's 'kitchen cabinet' of civil servants. Much drier, but good for the nuts and bolts of administration, is J. A. Oliver, *Working at Stormont* (Dublin, 1978). Often over-looked, but containing excellent material from politicians, civil rights activists, and a leading civil servant, is W. H. Van Voris, *Violence in Ulster: An Oral Documentary* (Amherst, 1975). O'Neill's economic advisor, Tom Wilson, wrote a general survey of Northern Ireland, *Ulster: Conflict and Consent* (Oxford, 1989) which includes his memories of O'Neill and his administration. For a view of 'Civic weeks' from a supportive catholic perspective, see Maurice Hayes, *Minority Verdict* (Belfast, 1995). Andrew Gailey utilises the copious correspondence of Jack Sayers, editor of the influential *Belfast Telegraph* and a close O'Neill ally, to produce an outstanding study of the period: *Crying in the Wilderness* (Belfast, 1995).

Analytical guides to the historiography may be found in John Whyte's magisterial *Interpreting Northern Ireland* (Oxford, 1990) and John McGarry and Brendan O'Leary's controversial and brilliant, *Explaining Northern Ireland* (Oxford, 1995).

The O'Neill years feature in virtually every general history of the 'Troubles', as so many have been written, it is impossible to include even the best of them here. Michael Farrell's *Northern Ireland: The Orange State* (London, 1976, 1980), written from a left-republican point of view, remains highly stimulating. An early canonical work, since updated and still without peer is Paul Bew, Peter Gibbon and Henry Patterson, *Northern Ireland 1921–1994* (London, 1995). Both Patterson and Bew have added further to our knowledge of the period since: see Paul Bew, *Ireland: The Politics of Enmity* (Cambridge, 2007) and Henry Patterson, *Ireland since 1939* (Oxford, 2007). Paul Dixon interestingly applies the theory of 'modernisation' to O'Neillism in his *Northern Ireland: The Politics of War and Peace*, 2nd edn (Basingstoke, 2008). Thomas Hennessy, *The Origins of the Troubles* (Dublin, 2005) is strongly argued and valuable. Graham Walker's essay on 'Politics since 1960' in Liam Kennedy and Philip Ollerenshaw's *Ulster since 1600* (Oxford, 2013) briefly and effectively puts the period into context.

There have been only two books specifically dealing with O'Neill's premiership. David Gordon's *The O'Neill Years: Unionist Politics 1963–1969* (Belfast, 1989) is polemical, bracing and wonderfully comprehensive within quite a short span. Even though it was written before the release of government documentation, its skilful use of copious newspaper resources makes it an invaluable work still. Marc Mulholland's *Northern Ireland at the Crossroads: Ulster Unionism in the O'Neill Years* (Basingstoke, 2000) is a survey of Unionist politics in general, so is not quite superseded by this current volume. Feargal Cochrane's essay, '"Meddling at the crossroads": the decline and fall of Terence O'Neill within the Unionist community' in Richard English and Graham Walker (eds), *Unionism in Modern Ireland* (Dublin, 1996) is an insightful, critical view. Sabine Wichert's 'Terence O'Neill and his politics', in Juergen Elvert (ed.), *Northern Ireland, Past and Present* (Stuttgart, 1994) is the best short introduction. Marc Mulholland's and 'Assimilation versus segregation: Unionist strategy in the 1960s', *Twentieth Century British History* vol. 2, no. 3 (Sept. 2000) and 'Why did unionists discriminate?', in Sabine Wichert (ed.), *From the United Irishmen to Twentieth-Century Unionism: A Festschrift for A. T. Q. Stewart* (Dublin, 2004) attempted theorised overviews on O'Neill's era. Two early books by a contemporary and very well informed local journalist are extremely helpful for the O'Neill years: *Fifty Years of Self-Government* (Newton Abbot, 1971) and *Drums and Guns: Revolution in Ulster* (London, 1970), both by Martin Wallace.

General surveys of the Ulster unionist Party include John F. Harbinson's *The Ulster Unionist Party 1882–1973* (Belfast, 1973). The potted biography of O'Neill is very insightful. Graham Walker's *A History of the Ulster Unionist*

Party (Manchester, 2004) is excellent. His convincing thesis is nicely summarised by the subtitle: 'Protest, pragmatism and pessimism'. Steven Bruce's study of *Paisley* (Oxford, 2007) is the best available.

Peter Rose, *How the Troubles Came to Northern Ireland* (Basingstoke, 2000) and Geoffrey Warner, 'Putting pressure on O'Neill: the Wilson Government and Northern Ireland', in *Irish Political Studies* (2005), it seems to me, far overstate the ability of a benign British government to mould Northern Ireland's politics to its will, but they have much useful information and bracing argument. Bob Purdie's *Politics in the Streets* (Belfast, 1990) is still the definitive book on the civil rights movement, but Simon Prince's *Northern Ireland's:'68* (Dublin, 2007) focus on the illusions and mistakes of the radical activists, if over-egged, is a useful corrective to sentimentality. For the Nationalist Party and the Northern Ireland Labour Party respectively, see Brendan Lynn, *Holding the Ground* (Aldershot, 1997) and Aaron Edwards, *A History of the Northern Ireland Labour Party* (Manchester, 2009). A very fine study of the republicanism in the period is Matt Treacy, *The IRA, 1956–69* (Manchester, 2011).

Index

Abyssinia 5
Adams, Gerry 96
Ahoghill 9–10, 13
Anderson, Albert 66, 76, 80
Andrews, John 26, 84
Anti-Partition League 11

Bailie, Robin 72–3
Bateman, Cecil 17, 39
Bew, Gibbon and Patterson 24
Bloomfield, Kenneth 17, 63, 86–7
Boal, Desmond 47–8
Bogs 40, 47, 48
Bond, James Bond 7, 39
Boyle, Louis 73
Bradford, Roy 45, 66–7, 74
Brett, Charles 56
Brooke, John 76
Brookeborough, Lord 11, 14, 16, 23, 24, 50, 91
    resignation 26
Bunting, Ronald 61
Burns, Joe 78
Burntollet ambush 65, 81–2

Cameron Commission 68–9, 93–4
Callaghan, James 83
Campaign for Social justice (CSJ) 53, 88

Campbell, Peter 76
Carson, Edward 45–6
Chapel-Gate Election (1949) 11, 19
Chichester-Clark, James 49, 83, 84–5
Civic Weeks 54–7
Cochrane, Feargal 57
Cole, John 15, 87
Colville, John "Jock" 7–8, 87
Cooper, Ivan 78
Copcutt, Geoffrey 33
Currie, Austin 56, 58
Craig, William 10–11, 19, 26, 30, 31, 32, 49–50, 63, 83
    and Civil Rights movement 59–60, 62
    sacked by O'Neill 65
    and Crossoads Election 70, 74–5, 78
    and Vanguard 92, 95
Craigavon See New City
Cromac Square riot (1966) 44
Crossroads Election (February 1969) 70–9, 81–2

Derry Citizens Action Committee (DCAC) 60–1
Devlin, Bernadette 82
Devlin, Paddy 78
Diamond, Harry 78

Diefenbaker, John 18
Divis Street Riot (1964) 38

Economic Plan 30
Education Act (1947) 13
Elizabeth II 45–6, 90

'Faceless Men' 34
Farrell, Michael 79
Faulkner, Brian 10, 19, 26–7, 31, 32,
    35, 39, 48–50, 54
    and Civil Rights movement 60,
        61–2
    split with O'Neill 68, 69–70, 73,
        76–7
    fails to succeed O'Neill 83, 85
    and Sunningdale 92–3, 95
Fitt, Gerry 53, 59
'Five Point Programme' (November
    1968) 62, 81
Flags and Emblems Act (1954) 37

Geraghty, Tony 71
gerrymandering 19, 33–4, 36, 55, 57,
    59
Giant's Causeway 27, 29
Gordon, David 17–18
Governor of Northern Ireland 26,
    45
Grant, William 14

Hall Report 24
Hamilton, Marquis of 75
Harland and Wolff Shipyard 21, 35,
    61
Hennessey, Thomas 80
Hume, John 69, 78, 90, 96
Ireland Act (1949) 14, 60, 61, 92

Irish Republican Army (IRA) 5, 19,
    22, 39, 43, 78, 86, 92, 97

Kennedy, John F. 27
Kilfedder, James 38

Long, William 83
Leeway 22
Lemass, Seán 16, 39–43
Lockwood Committee 30, 33–4

Malley, Jim 17, 84
Mater Hospital 57
Matthew Plan 25, 32
McAteer, Eddie 34, 39, 41, 52,
    59, 78
McCann, Eamonn 58
McCluskey, Conn 88
McCluskey, Patricia 88
McGuigan, Brian 71
McNeil, Mary 72, 73
Molyneaux, John 96
Morgan, William 49, 70, 72
Murphy, John A. 96

Nationalist Party 27, 30, 41, 52, 54,
    56, 69
NICRA (Northern Ireland Civil
    Rights Association) 54, 59, 63
Nixon, Robert 34
Northern Ireland Labour Party
    (NILP) 12–13, 23–4, 30, 35, 54,
    56, 72, 78
Northern Ireland Problem, The (1962)
    37
New City (Craigavon) 25, 32–3
New Ulster Movement (NUM) 71–2,
    89

One Man, One Vote 59, 62–3, 68, 83
O'Neill, Anne 9–10
O'Neill (Whitaker), Jean 6–7, 8, 39, 48
O'Neill, Phelim 83, 89
O'Neill, Terence
  personality 48
  autobiography 4, 13–14, 90–1
  geneaology 1–4
  youth 4–6
  anti-appeasement 6, 45, 48
  political ambitions 6
  world war two experience 6–8, 10
  marriage 6–7
  elected to Bannside 12–13
  favours Home Rule for Scotland
    14, 89
  as Minister of Finance 15
  Pottinger Speech 24–5
  becomes Prime Minister 26–7
  transforming the face of Ulster
    28–32, 35–6
  meeting with Lemass 39–43
  bans UVF 44
  'coup' attempt of 1966 47–9
  Corrymeela address (1966) 51–2
  meetings with Harold Wilson 35,
    53–4, 61
  response to Civil Rights
    movement 60–3
  'Ulster at the Crossroads'
    broadcast 63–4, 71
  appeals to catholic vote 70–1,
    77–9
  contest for Bannside (1969)
    74–5, 79
  resignation 82–4
  in House of Lords 89–90
  Irish Presidency 90
  on Sunningdale 94
  his aims 81
  as a technocrat 17, 31–2
  his internationalism 18, 27, 56
  self-Help 18–19, 28, 54
  work ethic 15–16, 17
  hobbies 9, 16
  passion for politics 16
  relations with civil servants
    16–17
  attitude to catholics 9–10, 28,
    79, 87–8
  relations with Unionists 47–8, 50
  Ulster at the Crossroads (book)
    86–7
  on the monarchy 46, 90
  as Anglo–Irish 4
  his pride in his Gaelic inheritance
    4
  and Irish unity 41–2
Orange Order 2, 13, 19, 32, 41

Parker, Dehra 15
PEP (Programme to Enlist the
  People) 54–7
People's Democracy 59, 65–7, 78
Paisley, Ian 10, 11, 13, 15, 19–20, 38,
  89, 96
  'O'Neill Must Go' campaign 40–1,
    49, 58
  1966 notoriety 44–7
  Bannside contest (1969) 74, 79
  and DUP (Democratic Unionist
    Party) 93, 95, 97
Plantation of Ulster 1
Porter, H. Archdale 80
Porter, Norman 13
Portadown Parliament 70, 75–6, 78

Presbyterian General Assembly
(1966) 44–5
Prince, Simon 80
Pro-O'Neill unionists 71–3, 75–7, 78

Second University 30, 33–4
Shane's Castle 5
Simpson, Robert 74
Special Powers Act 44
St Angelo Affair (1967) 49–50

Taylor, John 80
trade unions 31
Trimble, David 97

unemployment 21–2
Ulster Unionist Party (UUP) 12, 14,
47–50, 69, 70, 73–4, 79–80, 91
Ulster Volunteer Force 3, 43–4
Unionist (newspaper) 3, 47
United Irishmen 2

Walker, Brian 71
Warnock, Edmund 15, 26–7, 31
West, Harry 49, 76
Westminster, Duke of 76, 80
Wilson, Harold 42, 53–4
Wilson, Thomas 30, 53
World War Two 6–8, 10–11